LAIUS

A Play In Five Acts

JOHN WRIGHT

APS BOOKS
Yorkshire

APS Books,
The Stables Field Lane,
Aberford,
West Yorkshire,
LS25 3AE

APS Books is a subsidiary of the APS Publications imprint

www.andrewsparke.com

First published worldwide by APS Books in 2023

INTRODUCTION

I have always had an interest in the theatre and in my early twenties read and loved Greek Tragedy made accessible to me via the Penguin Classics series. My favourite play was Sophocles, *Oedipus Rex*. According to many scholars Sophocles, the Greek Dramatist who lived from 497-496 BC, was one of the greatest dramatists of all time. Aristotle, in his book *Poetics,* which deals with Greek Tragedy, often used examples from Sophocles plays, to define what Greek Drama should be. For some, Sophocles' tragedy, *Oedipus Rex* (also called Oedipus Tyrannus or Oedipus the King) is considered to be the greatest play ever written[1].

I loved reading *Oedipus Rex* so much so that I created my own 'transliteration' of it, which consisted of reading several copies of the play by different translators and then writing my own version from the gist of my understanding. Sadly my copy is lost, there were only a few produced and it was all done on a typewriter, so no computer files to save or back-up!

In 1981 Peter Hall directed Tony Harrison's version of *The Oresteia,* a play by the Greek dramatist Aeschylus (525 BC - 456 BC) at the National Theatre. This was a landmark production using music and masks, in an attempt to recreate the wonder and mystery of Greek Drama.

Reading more of Aeschylus's work I learned about his lost play *Laius*[2]. Apparently, there are a few lines scattered here and there of the original play of *Laius* but these amount to nothing more than tiny fragments and assorted odd lines. Regardless, the idea of a lost play had caught my imagination, and I began to explore the myths surrounding Laius and soon devised a scheme whereby my play would end at the death of Laius, killed by Oedipus and just before Sophocles takes up the story of Oedipus in *Oedipus Rex*. (The main difference is the death of Laius related in *Oedipus Rex* happens at a crossroads whereas in my play it happens in the palace.)

This play took me six years to write. It was begun in 1982 and completed in August 1988. I was also holding down a full-time job at the time. Not understanding the full complexity of Greek Drama proper I decided to write in a form and style I was more familiar with – Shakespearian drama. The play is written mainly in blank verse, which sometimes, as in Shakespeare's plays, uses rhyming couplets to end scenes. It consists of five acts and was devised and written with the intention that it would be performed on a blank stage. (I also did consider that it may well be performed by an all-male cast in the manner of

---

[1] This play can be found in the Penguin Classic, *The Theban Plays* by Sophocles along the two other plays in the trilogy *Oedipus at Colonus*, and *Antigone*. All three concern the fate of Thebes during and after the reign of King Oedipus.
2 There is also apparently a lost play of *Chrysippus* by Euripides.

i

traditional Greek drama and Shakespeare.) Part of the style is to use personification, so in the opening scene (Act 1 Scene 1) Cretheus[3] says:-

> 'Lest **Hope** desert and, **Fear** take refuge there."

Hope and Fear being clear examples of the use of personification.

The Story

My version of the play is compiled from various Greek Myths that dealt with the lives and actions of key characters in the play. My main sources at the time were Robert Grave's *The Greek Myths* in the two volume Penguin Edition, and *Lempier's Classical Dictionary*. Often, I read more than one version of the original story and chose the version or combined versions to suit my overall intention in making my play end, where Sophocles' *Oedipus Rex* begins.

The names and characters are all taken from Greek Mythology where their stories can be found. As with all myths there is often more than one account of the antics of the character, and their 'life' stories have many variants. I am no scholar and have shaped the various accounts to suit my own version of the tale in line with the dictates of my imagination.

The outline myth of Laius relevant for the play.

Laius was the king of Thebes, son of Labdacus, and father of Oedipus. After his father's death Laius was placed under the guardianship of Lycus.
Amphion and Zethus, murdered Lycus and usurped his throne, causing Laius to take refuge with Pelops[4] in the Peloponnese. While in the Peloponnese Laius fell in love with the illegitimate son of Pelops, Chrysippus and carried him off in what some accounts refer to as the first act of homosexuality.

Hippodamia the second wife of Pelops, feared that Chrysippus would succeed Pelops to the throne rather than one of her sons, and so stabbed the illegitimate son of her husband, using a sword owned by Laius. The stab wound did not cause immediate death, and Chrysippus was able to exonerate Laius before he died. Although my account does not address the exoneration.

After Amphion and Zethus died, Laius returned to Thebes, and ascended the throne of his father and married Jocasta. The oracle of Delphi foretold Laius that he would die by his son's hands, so Jocasta and he avoided any intimacy until one night Laius got drunk and lay with this wife. She became pregnant with Oedipus.

---

[3] *Lempier's Classical Dictionary* will give background detail of all the main characters, and I suggest one refers to it for more details.

[4] Pelops was king of Pisa in Elis, and from him the great southern peninsula of Greece was believed to have derived its name Peloponnesus; (*A Dictionary of Greek and Roman biography and mythology, Pelops (tufts.edu)*

After he was born, Laius fearing the words of the prophecy, pierced the ankles of the boy with spikes, and gave him to one of his herdsmen with orders that the boy should be left upon Mount Cithaeron. The boy was found by a herdsman employed by King Polybus of Corinth, who took him back to his master. Polybus and his wife, Periboea, were childless, and Periboea cared for the child as if it was her own, and because of his damaged feet, the king and queen called "their" new son Oedipus[5].

The oracle of Delphi had also prophesied that Oedipus would kill his father and marry his own mother. Hearing this, Oedipus vowed that he would never return to Corinth, to what he thought was his native land and his real parents. Instead, Oedipus travelled to Thebes.

On the way to that city he encountered his real father Laius, and in a fight over the right-of way killed him, without either party knowing the identity of the other person. (My play varies from that account in that Laius is killed in his own court. Sophocles uses the original account that Laius is killed by Oedipus on the road between Corinth and Thebes.)

---

[5] The injured feet as the source of Oedipus' name has been disputed by scholars.

CHARACTERS

Oedipus Captain in Pelops' camp (but really a son to Laius long supposed dead).
Oedipus believed he was Polybus' son (Polybus was the king of Corinth). He has come to Thebes to help Pelops in his war against Laius.

Country of Thebes

Laius	King of Thebes
Jocasta	his wife
Lysias	Friend and companion to Laius
Proteus	Captain in Laius's army.
Cretheus	Captain in Laius's army.
Pelias	Captain in Laius's army.
Lambrus	Foolish cook in Court of Thebes
Pitheus	Foolish cook in Court of Thebes

Servants etc.

■■■

Country of Paphlagonia

Pelops	King of Pisa in Elis.
Chrysippus	Son of Pelops by his first wife.
Hippodamia	Second wife to Pelops
Livia	Handmaiden to Hippodamia. (Also girlfriend to Thyestes).
Lucien	Messenger and lover to Queen Hippodamia
Atreus	Son to Hippodamia
Thyestes	Son to Hippodamia
Arrian	Serving wench and girlfriend to Atreus
Watchman	A Watchman in love with Hippodamia

■■■

Tiresias	Wise, blind sage renowned throughout Greece.
Nileus	Boy servant and 'eyes' to Tiresias.

ACT 1 SCENE 1

Battlefield, night, thunder and lightning, wind and rain, shouts skirmishes, on stage Captains Cretheus, Pelias, and other soldiers.

CRETHEUS: Stand to!
Form up a square. Look ready and alert!
The King is any moment this way due.

PELIAS: King Laius?
What brings him out on such a night as this?
I would have thought soft sheets and wanton boys
Would keep him safe indoors.

CRETHEUS: He comes to view the battle. Cheer the men.
Ten years of bloody war needs constant care,
Lest Hope desert, and Fear take refuge there.

PELIAS: (SHOUTS) Form up! Look Sharp!
It is not Fear that stalks so boldly through our ranks,
But Discontent.
My men grow weary with this endless war.
These night assaults are nurturing dissent,
And angry voices question why we fight.

CRETHEUS: Aye, well they might.
Who would, for pointless Pride, brave such a storm?

(Thunder and lightning.)

PELIAS: *(Shouts)* Look sharp!
This angry sky has allies in the town
Where civil strife and turmoil bang their drum.
Why, fifty of my fittest men were ta'en
To quell a rowdy mob of farmer's sons;
Who argued - in good sense that I could tell -
That where we fought despoiled the soil below
And made a barren waste of fertile land.
My men were so reluctant in their role
- They're fighting men, not keepers of the peace -
That had those youths not wearied and dispersed,
Would soon have rallied with them in their cause.

1

CRETHEUS: 'Tis a sad and sorry day
When peasants rise rebellious 'gainst their King.
This country boils and festers like a sore,
That aches to lance its seamy, acrid pus,
And rid itself of pain.
Too long this war has raged. The people cry for peace
And pray to have their country whole again.
But Laius keeps them servile to his whim,
And we must battle for the pride of Kings.

PELIAS: But look! See where he comes:
A knight in jet-black armour. Bold and dark!
And there, upon his right, young Lysias,
His favourite from the court.

CRETHEUS: Here comes the King. Stand to!

(Enter King Laius with Lysias and attendants)

LAIUS: Pelias. Cretheus. How goes the war this night?

CRETHEUS: Most noble King
This storm makes all our efforts seem but naught.
The gods hurl down their lightning on our heads
While Zeus's mighty laugh unseams the sky.
And we, with mortal fury, raise our swords
To smite the vanished shadows of our foe.

LAIUS: The gods make war
And mock our human frailty with their sport.

PELIAS: Some unpurged crime must lie behind this storm.
We've offered up libations, chants and prayers,
But nothing seems to satisfy their wants.

(Laius moves aside)

LAIUS: *(Aside)* Blood seeks blood.
This flashing sky is boiling with revenge,
But I'll not let it win.

(He moves back)

How are the men, still eager for the kill?

CRETHEUS: Oh most indeed! Our spirits are not low.
              Our Captain Proteus…

PELIAS: … 'The Bloody Scourge!'

CRETHEUS: (*Continuing*)…Is like a Lion when he urges on
              In each renewed assault his hungry pride
              Such that the scattered entrails of our foe
              Fly skyward at the roaring of his sword.

PELIAS: But they, likewise, are not without their brave.
              From Corinth comes a man …

CRETHEUS: …Nay! Beardless youth!

PELIAS: (*Continuing*)…Who fights as brave as men with twice his year
              Encouraging the Paphlagonian file.

CRETHEUS: Wild Oedipus, they call him - Tiger Wild!
              He leads his frenzied troops in loud attack
              And claws the very armour from our back!

LAIUS: Good Cretheus, your valour does you proud.
              You men are fair and honest that you can
              In loving terms so flatter those you fight.
              It seems by this report we're ev'nly matched.

CRETHEUS: Indeed tis true.
              We bang our heads together in this roar,
              But neither side makes Victory his prize.
              Regard the field, an impasse, that deceives.
              We ride upon a crest that seems at first
              To gain some vital headway in the fray,
              But then our roles reverse, and like a wave,
              We duck and bob upon the self-same spot,
              Wasting our fury on the waning tide.

              (*Thunder and lightning*)

LAIUS: (*Aside*) Is there no end to this?
              I thought by night-time fighting we would gain,
              What in the daylight's brightness was denied.

              (*thunder lightning and skirmish*)

              What's that? Some motion on the field?

3

Was that a child?
(shouts) I'll breed no Patricide!

(lightning)

Cursed lightning! For its light but partially shows
The lie of all our land in its bright blue.
It turns to shadow what has solid form,
And makes from shadow what has none at all.
(shouts) Are we to be deceived by formless forms,
And led astray by phantoms of the night?

(lightning)

These fires of heaven conspire to foil my plans
While evil spirits wreak some foul revenge.

(thunder)

(shouts); I'll heed no lofty sentence from your lips,
But seek my own salvation with this sword!

CRETHEUS: *(aside to Pelias)* The king is wild tonight.

PELIAS: *(to Cretheus)*
He has been wild, since first we broached this fight.

LYSIAS: Good Sir. You grow distracted. Calm your mind.
The men are most distressed by this display.

LAIUS: This curs'd rain floods o'er my sleepy eyes
And drowns my very vision at its source.
I cannot see the field. We shall retire.

(Proteus approaches)

PROTEUS: *(off)* AHOY!

LAIUS: Who's there?

PELIAS: Stand firm!

(Enter Proteus with a muddy prisoner - Lucien)

PROTEUS: Good Captains all! A present for the King!

4

CRETHEUS: Hail Proteus!

LAIUS: Welcome to our ranks good Captain.
               Your fame is like a spur to all our men,
               And urges them to action 'gainst our foe.
               You are most welcome. What's this?

CRETHEUS: What wretched, toad-like creature have you brought?

PELIAS: Is it a man?

CRETHEUS: Methinks it smells more like a corpse,
               That rots and festers on the rancid field.

PROTEUS: My liege, King Laius, this filthy prole,
               Who finds our mud congenial to his knees,

               (pushes the prisoner onto the ground)

               Wishes to have audience with you.
               He crossed our lines and begged that he be spared
               Commanding us to take him to the King.

LAIUS: A haughty knave. Who sent you - King Pelops?

LUCIEN: Hippodamia; my mistress and my Queen.

LAIUS: Hippodamia!
               That foul usurper of the female form!

LUCIEN: My Lord, I was commanded seek you out
               And give you this - a letter in her hand -
               Which has some bearing on this futile war.

LAIUS: Futile war!
               You make a kingly judgement in that scoff.
               We'll read this at our leisure, when the light's
               More truly in accord with what it lights.
               Not trusting Night with tasks beyond its ken.

LUCIEN: No. No, my liege. No! It must be read at once.
               The contents are too vital to delay.

LAIUS: You command me?

LUCIEN: Oh no, great King; forgive a humble man.

I am a servant - ordered to obey -
I've not discharged my task until you've read.

LAIUS: Your anxious face betrays a depth of fear.
Does Pelops know his wife scrawls out her mind,
Upon the face of this imperfect scroll?

LUCIEN: Oh no my Lord. 'Tis known to you alone.

LAIUS: Hippodamia! Husband killer!
Torturer of slaves! Your mistress is a witch!

(He grabs his throat)

Was it you who held the poisoned cup
That felled her former husband in his prime,
Or robbed her sleeping father of his life?

LUCIEN: ...No! No!

LAIUS: ...And now she turns her venomed thoughts to me.
How do we know this note does not contain
Some foul bubonic spell to cause my death?

LUCIEN: No. I beg you. 'Tis not so!
She sends you some solution to this war.

LAIUS: What!
She's won the war already for our side,
By curdling old King Pelops with her brew?
Ha!
Go. Bring up a light that I may read.

(Exit a servant)

Your mistress is a curse on all she meets
The cunning consort of untimely death.

(Enter a servant bearing a fiery brand)

Here.
Lysias, come. Step aside and read.
Your heart is young and pure, her spell
Will find no easy dupe in you.

(Laius holds the torch while Lysias reads. They stand apart from the others)

LYSIAS: *(reading)* "Most Noble King.
I sue to meet you in a secret place
That we may form a peace between our states.
This long redundant war now harms us both
And would be better ended than maintained.
(We can, by mutual favours, find a way
To benefit ourselves in such a scheme.)
The manner and the means we'll yet devise
When we have met and come to some accord.
My servant here will show where we can meet
He knows the time and place of my appoint.
I remain, the ever-humble servant of your reign,
Hippodamia. Queen of Phrygia."

LAIUS: Queen of Phrygia?
She fails to note that country has a King.

LYSIAS: This is a blatant insult to your crown.

LAIUS: Or else a cunning trap. Here, let me read.
I like not "...mutual favours..." nor the tone
Of "...when we've met and come to some accord.".
These crooked ink-starved letters show her thought.
See, between these tattered lines she's used the blot.
What dark, unwholesome mischief did she write,
That needed such a scoring to erase?

LYSIAS: Do not distract yourself with this.
The men are waiting, you must show them strength.

LAIUS: And here,
"The manner and the means we'll yet devise."
Am I but some dumb servant in her eyes,
Who needs to be reminded of his place?
She'll rue the day she ever wrote these lines.

LYSIAS: Good Sir. Put off this frantic rage.
You cannot hold such fits before the men.
It is unseemly and engenders fear.
Control yourself! Think no more of this note,
But cut its ugly cancer from your breast.
Come. We must away.
This night becomes too stormy for our good.

LAIUS: Sweet Lysias,
              Your gentle tongue corrects my straying thoughts.
              We'll speak no more the contents of this note.
              Come, let us away. Bring in that man,
              He'll fetch some sport before he meets his death.
              His mistress raves most madly in her fear,
              Our tactics touch the nerve-ends of their state,
              And cause their royal Queen to beg for help.
              Goodnight fair captains, may your watch be short
              And bring some fresh advantage with the dawn.

              (Exit King, Lysias, servants, attendants and Lucien.)

PELIAS: Would we could so to bed.

PROTEUS: Aye, right enough.
              But come, the battle rages. Hear our foe.
              Let's practice in the only art we know.

              (Exit all fighting)

                  END OF ACT 1 SCENE 1

ACT 1 SCENE 2

Hippodamia's chambers in the court of King Pelops.

HIPPODAMIA: Not returned?
              What mean you, "Not returned"?
              The sun is up. The battle's long since ceased,
              And yet, "He's not returned"?

WATCHMAN: Your majesty,
              I am a watchman, noted for my skill,
              And though I'm crippled, twisted and deformed,
              My eyes are sharp, my sense of hearing keen,
              And all my manly parts are still intact.

HIPPODAMIA: Get on!

WATCHMAN: Ghaarrr.
              All night long I've practiced at my art
              And stood upon the forefront of our ranks.
              I've watched your servant - Lucien - cross the field
              (A letter safely held within his shirt
              Against the raging fury of the storm).
              And there I've waited - 'till some minutes hence -
              When I was summoned, by your handmaid, to your side.
              And, through that long and dreary watch,
              He never once returned.

HIPPODAMIA: You lie! (*she slaps him*)
              You've slept throughout the zenith of the night
              And missed him. Slinking home to find your bed!

WATCHMAN: My eyes did never blink a wink of sleep!
              I've watched the lightning rend the rowdy sky.
              I've watched the blood-red dawn chase off the storm.
              I've watched our troops returning from that field
              - Where neither side advanced the smallest jot -
              And never once deserted from my post,
              Nor saw his poxy form returning hence.

HIPPODAMIA: Cur! (*she strikes him again.*)
              Go! Search his room.
              He's doubtless snoring soundly on his sheets.

(exit watchman)

Vile scum!
These imbeciles exhaust me with their lies
And judge me, while they rape me with their eyes!
Oh what a fool Ambition makes me seem
To draw me from the land I knew and loved
And cast me here on this barbaric shore,
Where now it mocks me with relentless toil.
Is this the price its ownership exacts;
To slay one husband (in a just revenge)
And gain a doting weakling in exchange?
How weary do I grow of Life's rebuffs
Which sap my strength and grind my spirit down.
Were there some way to end this endless pain!
Would that the past, lay buried, dead and done,
Not hourly rekindled in my brain.

(She sees a golden casket.)

Sweet Father,
Your ashes seem more precious to me now
Than all the power and wealth they once controlled
Which I, in youthful ignorance so craved,
I sacrificed your life to make them mine.
Oh how I rue the folly of that plot
- Which baser spirits urged me to obey -
To halt the gentle rhythm of your breath
And render thee, eternally to dust.
Oh had I but the power to give you life
I'd breathe again Life's breath into your lungs,
And swell those rosy cheeks with loving hue;
Make whole again, the man I little knew.
Sweet shameful tears, you do usurp your place
And stain - too late - this guilt inflicted face.
Why were you dry, when Death snuffed out his life?
Who dammed that flood which should have drowned me then?

(she weeps)

Oh that Hippodamia should come to this
The unwilling consort of a love-sick, doting, King,
Who showers his true affection on his son
And spurns my noble offspring with contempt.
Unjust, this choking fate that I endure!

10

Is this how gods teach mortals to obey?
Cease tears!
My majesty forbids this menial show!
(Self-pity steals the Action from our thought
And drains our dreams of sustenance and scope.)
I banish thee! ye salt filled drops of woe,
Congealed from spongy weakness and defeat.
Come breath,
And fill this heavy bosom with resolve.

(she takes a deep breath)

Ahh! There. I am a queen again.
My sons shall take revenge for all my pain
And rule the greatest empire known to man
Where Pelops, and King Laius, both shall be
The petty peons to my almighty strain.
But hush, my servant's not returned.
Perhaps he never made it cross the field
And lies face down upon the muddy earth,
My letter rotting with him on the ground.

(enter Livia)

LIVIA: Mistress.

HIPPODAMIA: Lucien?
                      Oh Livia, tis you. What news sweet child?

LIVIA: King Pelops bids you wait upon his side.

HIPPODAMIA: Oh let him wait!
                      I've more important matters here at hand.

LIVIA: What shall I say, he seeks a quick reply?

HIPPODAMIA: Tell him I'm ...cholic. Pale and weak,
                      And will attend upon him when I'm well.
                      Flesh out the message as your Fancy rules
                      Embellishing the details of my pain. But,
                      Construct your lie convincing to his ears
                      So Pity moves his jealous eyes to tears.
                      That way, at least, I keep him in my sway.

LIVIA   I shall.
                      My tongue has grown most nimble in this art

Through watching you, when sporting with the King.
Why yesterday you so controlled his moods
A puppeteer, quite baffled by your skill,
Demanded of a courtier, " Where's the strings?".

HIPPODAMIA: (*Laughs*) Foolish girl,
You should be beaten till you bleed.

(*They laugh and then she makes to leave*)

Wait! Where are my sons?

LIVIA   They're with their tutor, madam.
"Learning ancient law."

(*She says this in a gruff, deep, voice and mimics a doddery old
man - obviously the tutor.*)

HIPPODAMIA: Good.
Convey that fact to Pelops with your lie.
'Tis good that he should know how hard they strive.

LIVIA   I'll praise their manly efforts in such terms
That Heracles shall seem a eunuch's horn,
And Ares, but a withered, milkless, pap!

HIPPODAMIA: (*laughs*) Go, You wicked wretch.
These imbeciles must rue the day you came.

(*Livia curtsies and exits.*)

Sweet Livia, you, at least, still serve me well.
My only ally in this court of fools!

(*pause*)

That letter on the field could do me harm
If other eyes than Laius' chanced to read...

(*Enter Watchman*)

Well?

WATCHMAN: Your majesty.
His bed has not been slept in, nor disturbed;
And all was as he left it yesternight,

12

With not a drop of sweat to stink the air.

HIPPODAMIA: You yellow-bellied scum! How breathes you there
When he lies hacked and bloodied on the field?
Heard you no scream?

WATCHMAN: (*slowly, in disbelief*) Your Majesty?
The restless air was full of shouts and screams
Not least of all the Thunder's ugly roar.
To hear one scream, when thousands rend the air,
Is more than even I, can hope to hear.
Your majesty, we are at war.

(*Knocking - off*)

HIPPODAMIA: Go! Scourge the field.
Leave not one corpse in all that vale unturned,
Until you find his body, and my scroll.
At least do this thing well, you twisted fool!

(*more knocking*)

Go!

(*he bows*)

Go!

(*he exits by one door*)

(*she composes herself*)

Enter.

(*Enter Chrysippus*)

Chrysippus! What error brings you here?

CHRYSIPPUS: A noble errand, madam.
My father, hearing you were cholic,
Dispatched me here with these, to ease your pain.

(*He hands her a bunch of grapes.*)

HIPPODAMIA: The King's most kind.
And how are you, my noble stepson - Well?

13

CHRYSIPPUS: Indeed: I am well and touched by your concern.

HIPPODAMIA: Chrysippus!! Your life concerns me deeply.
              Come. Be not so stiff and formal in your stance,
              Relax, and free that tension from your limbs.
              Let's share together secrets from our thought,
              That we may learn to trust each other more.

CHRYSIPPUS: I have no secrets, that I'd gladly share.

HIPPODAMIA: Oh, come, come.
              Young men must have their secrets and their dreams.
              Are there no pretty girls who catch your eye,
              And drive your heart insane with thoughts of love?

CHRYSIPPUS: Madam.
              You know full well my love is for my kind,
              And women do not lead my heart astray.

HIPPODAMIA: Oh?
              I... I thought that was but juvenile delight,
              And would be shed when you became a man.
              My own two sons, contemporary with you,
              Have only eyes for girls, and see not boys,
              Thinking such affections most uncouth.

CHRYSIPPUS: My love of man is noble in its root,
              Drawing as it does on Friendship's base,
              And leading me towards some higher Truth!

HIPPODAMIA: Oh come, come, Chrysippus.
              True lovers fall in love to procreate,
              To father children, fill this world with joy.
              Does this urge touch you not - you selfish boy?

CHRYSIPPUS: Why do you rank mere fatherhood so high,
              As if this role alone could make us gods?
              The urge to procreate is crude and strong,
              Deriving all its power from Mother Earth,
              And makes us but the slaves of baser selves.
              To act like this, devalues our estate,
              Revealing us no better than a dog,
              Who, sensing some poor mongrel bitch on heat,
              Fulfils this chthonic function on the street.

14

HIPPODAMIA: You mock my suff'ring motherhood with this,
You vile, unnatur'l creature that you are.

CHRYSIPPUS: I meant no form of insult with my thought,
But merely state, what I believe is true.
Surely we have greater parts to play,
In Life's unfolding drama on this earth,
Than procreating species of ourselves?
A man must stand alone and be himself,
Not subjugate his wishes to the group!

HIPPODAMIA: These views of yours will undermine the State,
And cause us to forgo our right to rule.

CHRYSIPPUS: What care I for the State?
I hold a view of man, as he might be,
Free to rule each moment of his life,
Not pander to the whims of Kings and Queens.

HIPPODAMIA: You mock my functions, criticise all life,
Then seek to raise your failings to an art,
Because your 'love' perverts you to the truth.
Your kind should be extinguished at their birth,
To rid this earth forever of their curse!

CHRYSIPPUS: I'm sorry, that you see me as a curse,
I do not share your view,
But feel myself more noble in my love,
Than all my friends, who bind themselves, by lust,
To life-destroying roles beneath their worth.
Man, is a lofty creature, meant for more,
Than mere perpetuation of his spore.
Why spend one's life retracing well-worn steps
When every second offers such new goals?
We can, through our own efforts, be propelled
Beyond the shabby confines of our thought
To soar above the rich empyrean heights,
And dwell forever in a state of bliss!

HIPPODAMIA: Proud, foolish boy!
Because your love is tainted and impure,
You fantazise and build this world of dreams.
Be not too eager in this joyous mood,
Death, is always present here in Life,
And will snuff-out these childish dreams for good.

CHRYSIPPUS: Death?
Why mention Death, while we're exalting Life?

HIPPODAMIA: Poor childish boy!
You revel in this fantasy, while I reveal the facts.
We do not know when Death will come our way,
Or when His hand will rob us of our life.
See, how easily I crush this fragile form
And spill its vital juices on the ground.
(*she crushes a grape.*)

CHRYSIPPUS: I cannot comprehend your mind at all.
I seek to raise our spirits with great thoughts,
That we may soar together in delight,
While you gain satisfaction crushing grapes,
And choose to contradict each word I say!
Why do you always taunt me in this way?

HIPPODAMIA: Chrysippus!
I merely bring reality to bear,
On all the milky substance of your thought,
Which otherwise would leap this earthy world
And turn you into some weak, bookish, fop.
Your father is too lenient by far.
A boy like you should learn the martial arts,
And how to be a man, not lust and crave,
The filthy-minded pleasures of his kind.

CHRYSIPPUS: Desist! I will not hear you more!
You lacerate my feelings with your tongue.
I have no need to prove my worth to you.
My father sent me here to ease your pain,
Not suffer at your hands like some poor wretch,
Who you may use to your sadistic ends.
I've tried to bring you comfort with my thought,
But taste instead the venom of your tongue.
I know not why you hate me as you do,
But wish you would refrain from these attacks,
And treat me with the courtesy I'm due!

HIPPODAMIA: Chrysippus! I do not hate you,
But find your heady company too rich.
I'm used to meeting men who know their worth,
Not foppish boys, who contradict their birth.

CHRYSIPPUS: You'd mar the very sunlight if you could.

I have but one more duty to discharge,
Before I leave you, to the evil of your ways.
Tonight a feast for Oedipus is made,
He will become a Captain in our Guard,
And father wants you there in Royal attire,
To help present this honour when its due.

HIPPODAMIA: Huh! Oedipus.
Another filthy catamite like you.

(Pause: they stare at each other.)

CHRYSIPPUS: I will not be corrupted by your hate.

(He exits abruptly.)

(Hippodamia smiles, looks at a grape then slowly puts it in her mouth)

END OF ACT 1 SCENE 2

ACT 1 SCENE 3

The court of King Laius. Jocasta seated, sewing. enter Laius and Lysias

LAIUS   Lysias, Stem your speed. Come, give me weight.
        Your prowess in the bed has made me weak.
        My passing years, and aches from Love's delight,
        Cannot match your sprightly, youthful gait.
        Hah! Here's the prickly point of all my pain.

LYSIAS   Hold Sir! Your wife.

LAIUS   Ah! Jocasta!
        What wifely chore absorbs your widowed time?

JOCASTA   A trifle, Sir.
        Some humble stitchwork - nothing of account.

LAIUS   Here. We'll view your diligence. What!!
        An infant's shawl! I have forbid such things!

(He snatches the shawl.)

JOCASTA   It is not mine.
        I stitch it for a cousin full with child.
        It is a gift. A token of my love.
        Oh do not rend it so.

LAIUS   Your Love?
        You call this love, that can defy me thus?

(he shakes the shawl)

        No Childish things! I have forbid such things.
        You know as well as I the curse of Thebes.

JOCASTA   Oh Superstition's thrall.
        What harm can come of this? Tis but a gift;
        A simple shawl to warm an infant's form.
        Be sensible for once, and take my part,
        Instead of heeding prophecies of doom.
        My womanhood is mocked by your foul lust
        At least allow me comfort in my craft

18

	Where I may share, with sympathy and joy,
	The beauty of another's tender love.
	So long denied me, by this senseless curse!
LAIUS	My word is Law! I will not be defied!
JOCASTA	*(she kneels)* On bended knees I beg you, think again.
	Be lenient and merciful, my Lord.
	My empty hours have filled this fabric out
	Do not in rage destroy, what Patience here has formed.
LAIUS	*(He hands the shawl to Lysias.)*
	Here Lysias, what think you of this work?
JOCASTA	*(rises)* Humiliate no more!
	(she snatches the shawl back).
	No sodomite shall stand as judge o'er me!
LAIUS	*(He quietly takes the shawl again.)*
	Be silent cur. The boy shall have his say.
	Come Lysias, speak.
LYSIAS	But Sir, tis not my place.
LAIUS	Speak!
LYSIAS	I see no harm in sewing, Sir.
LAIUS	Indeed? Say more.
LYSIAS	The Lady's hand is neat, her touch is deft.
	Her art betrays a gentleness of thought.
	See here, these curls and spirals, twist and turn
	Like honeysuckle tendrils on a bough.
	And here, a five-starred pimpernel appears
	Its blood-red fury drained to purest white,
	Where silk supplants the vitalness of sap.
	And lo, a lover's knot, as yet undone,
	Betrays a heart that yearns for love to burn.
	This tells a pretty tale - though full of woe -
	Of one unloved, yet loving even so.
LAIUS	Brave boy. You've won your case.
	We'll make a politician of you yet.
	(aside) [Too brave by far.
	My ears must heed this winning tongue with care,
	Lest it usurp me with the smoothness of its speech.]

(He hands the shawl to Jocasta.)
Here wife, you may continue.

(Enter two Cooks, panting, they carry wooden spoons etc.)

Hah! Look, more smooth-tongued villains!
Here come two veteran scoundrels in that art.
So long they've served the servants of this State,
They know not when dissembling serves their ends,
Or when they serve the ends of those Dissemblers.
These drunk, unruly cooks, are so astute,
That when the dish is burnt, they blame the flame,
And then convince their hearer's of its guilt.
Good lying politicians every one.
Come Lysias, we'll have some sport awhile.
Lambrus. Pitheus. What drudgery descends upon us now?

LAMBRUS: Your majesty, we bring matter befitting your great ears.

LAIUS: My great ears?
               They're well proportioned, so I thought.

LAMBRUS: Oh indeed they are, such well proportioned ears.

PITHEUS: Such pretty, well proportioned, little ears.

LAMBRUS: Such little, pretty ears that suit your head.
               But yet, our news is larger than your ears,
               For though your ears be little...

PITHEUS: Aye, little and pretty.

LAMBRUS: Yet, they hear great things.

LYSIAS: *(To Laius)* A philosopher to be sure!

LAIUS: To the point man. Our ears- be they little, pretty, great
               Or well-proportioned - grow weary of your convoluted talk.

LAMBRUS: Your majesty, Pitheus and I are most irksome.

LAIUS: You are indeed, and tedious as well.

PITHEUS: Aye, Irked to the very sum, and tedious beyond belief.

LAMBRUS: True,
               And we can justify the cause of being tedious.

20

LYSIAS:	(*to Laius*) I'd like to hear it.
LAIUS:	To the matter.
LAMBRUS:	Your majesty, we come about an urgent matter. Which has made us both irksome and tedious.
PITHEUS:	Aye, tedious and irksome.
LAIUS	The matter.
LAMBRUS:	The matter, at its heart, is close your heart.
PITHEUS:	And yet, (*looking behind him. & trying to play down its scale.*) Not close enough to cause concern.
LAMBRUS:	But close enough to find its cause concerning.
LAIUS:	Concerning what? Be brief.
LAMBRUS:	Sir, in brief, and being brief is brevity's sole charm.
LYSIAS:	(*To Laius*) His wit is wondrous witty for a fool.
LAIUS	To the issue scoundrel! Be man enough to own your foolish acts.
LAMBRUS:	(*Fighting talk! To defend his honour, he starts waving the wooden spoon about*) I do not swerve, nor duck the issue underfoot, But hold it tightly in my open palm (*Opens his palm and drops spoon.*) I am your servant and dictate your needs, And bow before you with my head held high, And rail most loudly in my silent praise, Against those hungry mouths that hold broad sticks To beat (*Hits Pitheus with spoon, both feet off ground.*) Your Statutes down.
LAIUS	(*reels holding his head*) Ye gods! He mixes up his metaphors so well I feel like baker's dough, new-kneaded in a trough.
LYSIAS:	Speak plainly man.

21

Our ears are all disjointed by your talk.

LAMBRUS: *(he rolls up his sleeves.)*
To be plain and to the point,
without garnish or added salt....

PITHEUS: Or spice....

LAMBRUS: Or putting in false colouring......

PITHEUS: Or taste...

LAIUS Silence! Come to the point man!

LAMBRUS: In a word, Sir, and here again Brevity shall find me His sole
Champion and elongator...

PITHEUS: Sole champion and elongator...

*(Lysias puts his hands over his ears and ducks forward to avoid
the expected onslaught of words. Laius gives another stern look
and menacingly steps forward.)*

LAMBRUS: *(quickly, in fright.)* Good King,
Your wise and worthy policies are being misunderstood.

LAIUS: Ha! At last. Some matter we can chew upon.
Misunderstood, and why is that?

LAMBRUS: Why Sir, the matter is simple.

PITHEUS: Simple.

*(Pause. It suddenly dawns on Pitheus that he doesn't know what
Lambrus means so he looks at Lambrus who is still looking very
self-satisfied. he beckons desperately to Lambrus with his hands
trying to show him Laius is as puzzled as he is)*

LAMBRUS: Your people are simple, and there's the matter.

LAIUS: Then I too am simple,
For I fail to understand the meaning, the matter,
The content or the subject of concern.

LAMBRUS: Good Sir, lend me your ears.

LYSIAS: What! and have them filled with metaphors again.
             We'll hear no more of ears.

PITHEUS: But Sir,
             If you hear no more of ears, which hearing comes to hear
             Through; Why, then you will be deaf.

LYSIAS: I'd rather be deaf, than dumb as you!

             (*Enter a Sergeant.*)

LAIUS: Ha! Some sense at last.
             This Sergeant looks a man, who knows some truth.
             Speak Sir, we're eager for your news.

SERGEANT: Your majesty, A crowd of angry serfs,
             Demanding fairer prices for their grain,
             Have stormed the Western Gate,
             And rail the guards and curse your noble State.

             (*Lambrus & Pitheus slowly creep away.*)

LAIUS: But why are they so vexed?
             Know they not the country is at war?
             The price is fair. 'Tis all we can afford.

SERGEANT: Your Royal Cooks, who first met with the crowd,

LYSIAS: And now seem anxious to be out of sight...

SERGEANT: (*cont.*) ...endeavoured to explain the current price.
             But, being so inept at such a task,
             Soon lost control and set the crowd alight,
             Their verbal nonsense filling every ear.

LAIUS: Enough of ears.
             Come, I'll to the crowd and pacify their rage.
             Lysias, attend the shrine, Tiresias is due.
             Jocasta, take yourself within,
             You have no further business in the court.

             (*Exit Laius with the sergeant*)

             (*Jocasta and Lysias stand silent for a while*)

JOCASTA: Lysias, I thank you for your help.

I did you wrong to speak so harshly of your love.
I....

LYSIAS: I was not hurt. Your work is very good.
            And, by the way you hold it to your heart,
            Means more to you than just a simple shawl.

JOCASTA: Sweet youth, you are so gentle and so kind.
            Your eyes and mind are sharp and full of life.
            This... this soft and treasured article of cloth,
            Is all that I have left of my fine son...

LYSIAS: Your son? I've never knew you had a son!

JOCASTA: Oh. I've said too much!
            No Lysias! Ask no more.
            Forget what you have heard.
            Laius would destroy me if he knew.

LYSIAS: Be not afraid, your secret's safe with me.
            But tell me this, who was the sire?

JOCASTA: No! No more! Forget you ever heard.
            Oh foolish tongue, to utter what must never be revealed.

LYSIAS: (He comes forward and takes her hands.)
            Sweet lady, chastise yourself no more.
            My ears have never heard, nor does my mind suspect,
            That this is any other than a shawl,
            Or you, are else but virgin, as is told.
            Rest easy in yourself.
            I have no need of knowledge that's forbid.
            Come. We shall be friends.
            You've suffered long enough from lack of love.
            I cannot give you other than support,
            But this, I gladly will provide.

JOCASTA: Oh dear, sweet boy.
            Your kindness melts the outrage of my heart.
            These twenty years I've felt Rejection's smart,
            And lain in empty beds, my flesh intact,
            While Laius drank full measure of his lust,
            With cheeky, wanton boys, who'd plague the court,
            And treat me like some filthy, pox-filled, whore
            Who had no right to Love, or Lust's pure joy.
            For many years, alone, I've sought relief

24

By undertaking acts - best long forgot -
Which in my girlhood seemed a true delight
But paled, when Laius took me, on that night.

(Lysias reacts, hearing who the father is.)

(almost pleading.) A woman needs a man to make her whole,
And you can play, for me, that precious role.
Your friendship now, will prove a needful cure,
And flood with love, this desert I endure.

LYSIAS: Then I shall gladly play Hyperion's part,
               And send my healing rays to thaw your heart.

JOCASTA: And I'll play Spring to your, warm-summer light,
               And blossom to fruition in your sight.

(Enter Laius unseen)

LAIUS: *(Aside)* What's this, a plot behind my back?
               Has this young boy grown weary of my love,
               And seeks his satisfaction somewhere else?
               But no, he's not to women drawn.
               Yet, see how he holds her, comforts her, and soothes.
               This boy has many facets I've not seen.
               His form's divine and yet his mind is filth,
               Does Beauty thus corrupt what it should love?

JOCASTA: But Laius must not know of our intent.
               His mind is full of jealousy and rage,
               And will suspect the nature of our pact -
               Being so unknown to friendship without lust.

LYSIAS: He will not hear from my devoted lips.

JOCASTA: Nor mine. *(she kisses him)*

(Laius comes forward.)

LAIUS: Get you hence wife! I've issued one command.
               Do you intend defying every rule?

JOCASTA: I meant no harm.
               The boy has shown me kindness, that is all.

LAIUS: Go.

(Jocasta hurries off).

(Pause. Uneasy silence. He watches her depart, his back to Lysias.)

LYSIAS: Settled you the crowd?

LAIUS: Crowds are easy. Tis friends who settle last.

LYSIAS: I know not what you mean.

LAIUS: The crowd are happy now. I am their King,
And when I state the reason for our laws,
They willingly obey,
Not anxious to hatch plots behind my back.
Conniving with she-devils in such schemes.

LYSIAS: I too obey, and hold you in my heart,
Above the fickle feelings of this mob,
Or any false imaginings you have.

LAIUS: Obey?
The shrine has not been lit. The altar's unprepared.
What manner of obedience is this?

(Enter Tiresias, led by a beautiful young Boy.)

TIRESIAS: Harsh words! Harsh Words!
What welcome chaunt is this?

LAIUS: Tiresias! Most welcome sage!
Forgive my angry voice - some trifle of the court.

TIRESIAS: Trifles stir not storms within the mind
That need to vent their fury in such sound.
Your words assault this air with fear and rage
Like some unruly-bear leased from his cage,
And baited 'till he drop within the ring.

LAIUS: Forgive me - I meant you no offence,
My speech grew heated o'er some petty fault.

TIRESIAS: Our speech is but the echo of our thought
And shows most clearly what our feelings plot,
Revealing through its tone our heart's true state.

26

LAIUS: Good Sir,
            We lesser mortals (Kingly though we be)
            Live in cruder worlds, and harsher realms,
            Than those whose lives pursue a higher goal.
            We act in haste, expressing what we feel,
            In ugly words which rip the virgin air.
            When'er I find deceit or subterfuge,
            My temper leaps like flames annoyed with oil
            And vent's my Anger's fire in instant heat -
            Then cools at once, no embers left to chafe.
            Be well assured this matter is now o'er.
            Here, I'll be your guide. You are most welcome.

            (He takes his arm to lead him.)

TIRESIAS: Unhand me.
            I would not have a servant blind as you
            Lead me through the mysteries of life.
            I'll stand alone. *(To the boy.)*
            Go boy, I'll call you when I need.

LAIUS: Lysias, light the incense, fetch some softer seat,
            Our honoured guest has travelled many miles,
            To grace the humble trappings of our court.

            (Lysias and the boy exit.)

TIRESIAS: An old and withered man graces nothing.

LAIUS: Come sir,
            Your body is the temple of your mind -
            That mind so well renowned it makes men quake.

TIRESIAS: Who fears my mind, had best beware his own,
            For I own nothing, which he does not possess.
            All fear is but at root a fear of death,
            And death is but a change or shift in being.
            Why quake in terror at what soon will be
            All living forms perforce must rot and die.
            Who hides this truth will suffer for the lie!

            *(Re-enter Lysias, with two cushions. He places the cushions on
            the ground and lights the incense. Laius arranges the cushions.
            Lysias removes the torches and the room darkens - he exits.)*

27

LAIUS: Come. Sit. The place is all prepared.

TIRESIAS: This place is well prepared, but is your mind?
                Dame Future does not willingly reveal
                The subtle strands and structures of her course
                To those whose thoughts are full of jealous rage.
                Come, sit with me awhile,
                And calm that boiling lake of greed and hate,
                Which passes in this kingdom for a mind.

                (They sit in silence for a while - meditative then Tiresias chaunts a long deep "ahh" note held for a long time)

                Ahh!

                (after some time)

                Let the prophecy proceed!

                (Tiresias opens the bag he is carrying and very slowly and reverently takes out some tortoise shells. he chants the following.)

                Random Chance, and Destiny,
                Merge within these items three,
                Link the thoughts of he who quests
                With the mind that then must wrest
                The meaning from this hidden scheme,
                The meaning of this waking dream.
                Random Chance, and Destiny,
                Merge within these items three.
                AHH! HOO! KO!

                (He hands the shells to Laius.)

                Make your choice.

                (Laius slowly chooses three of the shells and hands these to Tiresias who very carefully feels them all over.)

                (Chants) NA-RO! TA-RO! BA-RO!

                (He shakes his head sagely)

                These shells are deeply grooved. You've chosen well.
                The reading will be true. Your question?

LAIUS: I have received a plea for peace.
                From Pelops' wife.
                Is there treachery involved?

                (Tiresias takes his time, he moves slowly and reverently he feels
                the shells)

TIRESIAS: The woman is treacherous; as all women are.

LAIUS: And is my life at risk?

TIRESIAS: No. Not your life.
                You have been told before; your son will take your life.
                Here it is writ, and here will it remain.
                Until that act befalls.

LAIUS: And of this peace, will it come to pass?

TIRESIAS: If you wish it so.

LAIUS: And there's no danger to my life?

TIRESIAS: You doubting man.
                Why, one and twenty years ago today,
                When you were new-make king of this proud land,
                You had me summoned here to ply my trade,
                That you might know the outcome of your life.
                I told you then, as I today have done,
                Your life is safe until your only son,
                Through patricide and passion lays you dead.
                Such is the case, and thus it will remain,
                Until this gory prophecy's fulfilled.
                You have no son, and thus far, are you safe.

LAIUS: Tiresias... I...

TIRESIAS: Your mind is anxious, restless and perturbed.
                What secret thoughts pass through that seething brain
                To course these wild contortions through your frame?

LAIUS: Tiresias, your prophecy is true!
                When, these many years ago, you made this known,
                I was, as yet, unmarried to my queen.
                Her hand was promised. (An affair of state
                Her father and my father both had formed,

Before I even stepped upon this earth.)
So, when we wed, I kept her womb intact,
Prophetically forewarned of what might chance,
And spent instead, my hot unruly seed,
On boys and youths who willingly complied.
Until one night, when roused by too much wine,
I stumbled, by mistake, into her room,
And there upon her virgin, pristine bed,
Made many hot assaults upon her womb,
'Till she and I, in ecstasy believed,
That all our lives had led to this one night.
Next day, Sobriety re-sharpened all my wits,
And I returned at once to loving boys
And crushed all vulgar rumours of that act,
Pretending that her Hymen was intact.
But Folly, being awake on that drunk night,
Had charged my seed with life, and filled her womb
With all the needful dictates for a child.
This child - a lovely boy
(My own, and yet my death, if you be true)
    - I had destroyed.

TIRESIAS: How?

LAIUS: My servant took the child into the hills,
And piercing both his feet with one long spike,
Hung him upside down upon a tree,
And left the mewling infant there to die.

TIRESIAS: And is he dead?

LAIUS: What infant could survive a fate like that?

TIRESIAS: Is he dead?

LAIUS: Presume no more!
The infant died on Cithaeron's far hill.
This mem'ry guilts me to the hilt. No more!

(Tiresias consults the shells again.)

TIRESIAS: NA-RO! TA-RO! BA-RO!
Your son will take your life!
This reading is not wrong.

LAIUS: Cease!

This reading mars the matter that you read.
No more I say! I'll hear no more.
Lights! Guard! Our meeting is now o'er.

(He jumps up shouting)

TIRESIAS: Proud, foolish, man. The meaning here is strong.
Your son shall take your life. This is not wrong!

(He brandishes a tortoise shell at Laius.)

(Enter Lysias with a torch followed by a Guard.)

LYSIAS: My lord, what's wrong?

LAIUS: Tis nothing! Nothing. Tiresias is leaving.
Guard. Fetch his guide.

(Tiresias gets up slowly, and wanders over to Lysias and touches his face gently)

TIRESIAS: A pretty, willing, boy I'll vouch.
And are you twenty?

LAIUS: Unhand that boy. You sick and scabrous man.
You've stunk this air with all your rancid breath.
Do not corrupt his youth with poisoned words.

TIRESIAS: Truth is Truth. It has no mortal price.
You cannot pacify, nor can you corrupt,
The Truth about your self my shells reveal.
The Truth is Truth. And you will face this Truth:
Your son shall take your life!

LAIUS: Begone old man before I take your life!

(The Boy comes running in and takes Tiresias by the arm and leads him off, followed by the guard.)

(Lysias runs to Laius and they hug comforting each other.)

LYSIAS: Come Sir.
The perfume of this air disturbs your mind.
The afternoon is young, let's to our beds,
Where we may lightly tease a trick or two.

31

(Exit Laius supported by Lysias.).

END OF ACT 1 SCENE 3

ACT 1 SCENE 4

A small, ornate, garden temple, in Pelops' palace with a fountain and a shrine also some gentle windchimes, which tinkle. discover Chrysippus sitting alone throwing pebbles into the fountain. Enter Pelops.

PELOPS: Dear Chrysippus, why sit you so alone?

CHRYSIPPUS: Oh Father, I did not hear you come.

PELOPS: Sweet child, what anguish sweeps your mind.
Your face is pale, your eyes are wet with tears.
Unburden here the torment of your heart.
What grieves you so? Your mother?

CHRYSIPPUS: My mind has ranged o'er many thoughts this morn,
Of what life is: and why it is we're born?
I've leapt among the firmament and seen,
The blazing vision of a life that's been:
A golden epoch, bathed in glowing light,
Where Life is sacred; Knowledge is a right!
A world in which no misery is known... *(pause)*
And yet,
I see by these deep furrows in your brow,
You follow not.
My mother? Yes. My mother's touched me too,
Her love is always with me in my heart.

PELOPS: Dear Child. My precious, only, child,
This garden shrine; this sepulchre to her;
That you should come and weep for her demise.
Your mother was an angel here on earth,
A creature full of light, and Life's delight.
She flitted unimpeded round my court,
Like some unseasoned butterfly, in flight,
Seeking out the sun before its time.
She was a joy, a treasure rich and rare,
Unique in all her attributes and skills.
And then you came,
More radiant by far than her pure form,
And gave us both, a wealth beyond compare.
Oh Chrysippus, I mourn your mother's loss,
I had this magic garden formed for her.
These three, long, years have seemed a lifetime's pain,

But she is gone, and you, at least, live on,
With all her perfect virtues still intact.
Do not be sad for her, my heart will burst.
Take comfort in the living, be alive!
Sweet Hippodamia loves you, like myself,
Grow fond of her, and heal this painful loss.

CHRYSIPPUS: *(very slowly and deliberately.)*
Dear Father,
You are a good, and kind, and simple man.
I love you greatly... love you close to tears,
And yet I cannot tell you what I feel;
Cannot share this pain which gnaws inside,
And stirs my thoughts in endless search for peace.
My mother was an angel, as you say,
And filled your court with light, where'er she went.
She gave to Life a richness unsurpassed,
A vision of what Living truly is.
I miss her sorely, and her endless love,
Which fed my growing years with such proud hope,
It left me unaware of Death's wide scope.
Who could believe that Life must end like that;
One day, alive and breathing, fresh and free,
The next, a rotting bag of blood and pus.
Thus Death will make foul garbage of us all!
And so my heated brain seeks on and on,
For some solution to this frailty - 'Life'.
And here I sit,
To tease some comprehension from the air.

PELOPS: Oh grieve not so but come away inside.
We'll soon find some distraction from these thoughts.

CHRYSIPPUS: This garden is the only place I know,
Where silent meditation soothes my mind,
Where I can come to terms with what has passed,
And contemplate the fate of all mankind.
I spend my lonely hours in here, at peace,
Oblivious to the world that lies beyond,
And draw great solace from this silent grove,
Where Time forgets His duty, in repose.
I'm lulled by all the magic of this place:
The gentle murmur of the water's fall;
The lilting tinkle of the windchimes' song;
The vibrant presence of my mother's love.
I come to study wisdom from the East,

34

Relayed by men who, passing through our court,
Display the rich composure of their thought,
And walk serenely through our troubled land.
I come to study views about this world,
Which ancient scrolls record as true and real,
And hint at strange solutions to our weal.
I come to scrutinize my private thoughts,
To challenge all the notions I assume,
To question what this life is all about,
And find some harbour from this sea of doubt.
But most of all, I come to sit in peace,
To bask within the balm of this pure place,
And feel the gentle silence of my thought.

PELOPS: Oh come away!
This musing here on life, befits you not,
And seems to contradict your tender years.
Come. My Hippodamia waits,
She'll shower you with love and ease your pain.
She is your mother, bosom to your heart.
Come join us now and soothe your o'er taxed brain.

CHRYSIPPUS: *(very considered and after a considerable pause, he stands.)*
You love your second wife, I never shall.
She is no friend of mine, nor loves me true;
Nor is a second mother to my needs.
We disagree - I cannot find the cause -
And seek at every chance to give her love,
But know she hates my presence through and through...

PELOPS: Sweet child! Do not speak thus!
You do abuse the privilege of youth.
She hates you not!
She is my wife, your mother, by that bond.
She cannot hate you!
I know she finds you difficult to know:
Your ways are... different from hers,
You brood a lot, and wander off alone,
Your mind is wrapt in thought, and oft engaged,
In thinking through ideas, no woman has.
You dwell in worlds, Imagination makes,
And lose all sense of urgency in life.
I too, am very fond of these abodes,
Of dreaming dreams of what the world might be,
Of how our lives should echo what we dream,
And fill our waking moments with delight.

35

But this is idle, and can never be,
So waste no further time in such pursuits.
Do not despair. She'll love you by and by.
She has two sons, and these she values first.
This is not strange, nor seems so out of place,
For I love you, and hold your value more,
Than ever I could value her two sons.
Yet they, to me, are... equal in my love.
She does not hate you! This I will not hear!
She is my lover, wife, and heart's repose.
She cannot hate you? You are my son!
No! No! You have misunderstood.
She cannot hate you?
Come. Come with me indoors.
(He wraps his arm around Chrysippus' shoulder.)
This morbid brooding on your mother's grave
Will agitate the senses from your brain.
She cannot hate you?
Come.
Oedipus, your mentor and your friend,
Is due to reach our court this afternoon,
He'll help dissolve this mood of inward gloom.

CHRYSIPPUS: *(slowly again.)*
It is not gloom that fills my aching mind,
But questions of the right's and wrong's of Life;
Of Motivation, Action, Love and Hate.
It is not wrong to question what we think!
I feel such stimulation in these thoughts,
These questions, 'Why we fear?', and 'Why we doubt?',
Which tear the very fabric of our being.
Above, I see an emptiness of space
So vivid and so vital in its depth
It shakes my tiny self-hood to the core.
It rattles all my fundamental hopes
And sends me spinning in a star-filled void,
Towards some universal, Endless, goal.
This is where our life is meant to lead,
Where all our thought, our mind, our being, belongs!
We are not simply bags and bones of earth
Confined to idle chatter here below,
But creatures from a realm beyond our thought.
We have a higher purpose in this life,
Which gods, and all our worship points us to.
Our life is endless, upwards, onwards, out!
I am not gloomy, when I'm in this mood,

36

But quaking on the edge of living flame,
Ablaze with all the fire of Perfect Being!

SHOUTS OFF: My Lord! King Pelops!"

PELOPS: I must go in. They wait for me in court.
              You do amaze me with your dizzy moods,
              And all these flights of fancy you adopt.
              Your mother - Hippodamia - has observed
              You need some relaxation from these thoughts.
              A first I could not fathom what she meant,
              But now I do.
              Young Oedipus, your strong and manly friend
              Will help you tread more harsher, firmer, ground.
              Be guided by his love.
              Be less inspired. More simple in your hopes,
              For life is long and difficult to bear
              And Visions lost, cause madness and despair.
              (Further shouts, off.)
              But now I must attend this pining court.
              (He kisses Chrysippus then exits.)

CHRYSIPPUS: *(shaking his head at his father's departure.)*
              What tragedies our mundane selves maintain.
              Why do we choose to wallow in this mud,
              When in one leap we can o'er-vault the sky?
              Our minds confine us to our weakest self,
              Contenting us with mediocre roles,
              And blinding us to Life's eternal goals.
              When will men ever learn how free they are?
              Oh Oedipus, I would that you were here,
              You share these views with me, and are my peer.
              I totter now 'tween madness and delight,
              And need a strong companion in my fight,
              To overthrow these slothful views of life!
              Together you and I shall yoke our love,
              And harness here on earth, what lies above!
              (He exits.)

              END OF ACT 1 SCENE 4.

ACT 1 SCENE 5

A chamber in the court of King Pelops, enter Atreus & Thyestes.

ATREUS: The Man's a fool!
Why should we study laws that don't exist?
His brain has addled with his passing years.

THYESTES: Imagine what his manhood must be like.

(Mimicking a tiny, flaccid prick with his finger. They laugh.)

ATREUS: Our mother's vast ambition ties us here.
I'd rather be out riding on my mare,
Than chained to dusty scrolls, and lifeless thoughts.

(Enter Arrian: a serving girl)

THYESTES: *(elbows Atreus)* I know what I'd rather be riding.

ATREUS: *(aside to thyestes.)* I'll warrant I can chafe her bit 'fore you.

THYESTES: *(aside to Atreus.)* Go to't and may the best man win.

ATREUS: Arrian, do you attend our mother?

ARRIAN: I do.

ATREUS: I do, Prince Atreus.

ARRIAN: Prince Atreus? You're less a prince than I am.
For all your mother is the Queen.

ATREUS: You'd never make a Prince,
You lack the princely virtues I display,
Being swollen in the wrong department.

(He mimics her breasts, and his penis.)

ARRIAN: At least I've not a swollen head like you,
Nor think my role more regal than it is.

ATREUS: You'd soon be moaning if my head was limp.

ARRIAN: If your head was limp, I'd certainly not moan.

THYESTES: A haughty wench! Come here! *(he grabs her arm.)*
               You say he's not a prince,
               But I, am I not Prince Thyestes.
               And have control o'er when my head is swollen or is limp?

ARRIAN: You're more a prince than him.
               Yet still a saucy knave,
               Who thinks himself beyond his true estate.

THYESTES: Atreus,
               I think this girl has something on her mind.

ATREUS: *(going forward.)* Nay. Something on her chest.
               She needs to make a clean breast of it.

               (he grabs hold of her bosom.)

ARRIAN: *(she slaps him.)* Unhand me cur! You'll get me wrong!

ATREUS: Unhand you? I'm no where near your hands.

               (He grabs her and kisses her. She pushes him back.)

ARRIAN: I'll scratch your eyes if you do that again.

ATREUS: I'd rather have you scratch my back.

               *(He grabs her again. They struggle and fall to the floor
               giggling.)*

               (enter Livia.)

LIVIA: Get up you fools; the queen is on her way.

THYESTES: Another wench, and this one's just as game.
               This place is surely but a fountain of delight,
               That spews forth virgins...

ATREUS: Virgins! That's a lie!
               She lost her precious maidenhead at twelve.

THYESTES: Yes, and well we know who pricked her bubble.
               (he pinches her.)

LIVIA: Saucy fellow! (*She slaps him*) I've got the measure of you.

ARRIAN: Aye, in inches too.
                (the girls giggle together.)

LIVIA: True. The smaller brother is much the bigger man.

THYESTES: You filthy slut!
                (He grabs Livia and kisses her, while Atreus chases Arrian.)

                (Enter Hippodamia.)

HIPPODAMIA: Boys! Boys!
                Your piercing shrieks and screams will wake the dead.

                *(They all scramble to their feet and look abashed, dusting
                themselves down.)*

ATREUS: Oh mama, we meant no harm.
                These girls here, led us on.

HIPPODAMIA: Come, Come, my child, your mama is not cross.
                (she hugs him to her and strokes his head.)
                At least you boys are manly in your play,
                Unlike that brat who dotes upon his kind.
                You girls have work to do?

ARRIAN: & LIVIA: *(They curtsey.)* *(Together)* Yes mam.

HIPPODAMIA: Well, set about your tasks.
                My sons were born for greater spoils than you.

ARRIAN: & LIVIA: *(Together)*   Yes Mam.

                (they curtsey and exit.)

HIPPODAMIA: Come Thyestes,
                Kiss your mama's lips and look not so abashed.
                Your blushing cheeks will shame the robin's breast.
                (She hugs them to her.)
                Ah children, offspring of my womb.
                One day, my chicks,
                If all my dreams come true - which I intend they shall -
                You'll be the kings of this,
                This,
                And all the other countries here around.

Yours all yours, to reign as you see fit,
Unhampered by the thoughts of petty men,
Who strive through weakness to placate the mob,
And sacrifice their sovereignty to serfs:
Make democratic nonsense of their right,
To be a king, and rule with all their might!
No! Not me! Not sons of mine! Here they'll reign supreme,
And show the world where Hippodamia thrives.
Boys? Boys? Rejoice!
Your pallid looks and gormless gaping mouths,
Are more befitting men condemned to death.
Did Mama frighten you? Come. You must not be afeared.
Why, even Chrysippus shows greater strength than you.
Come!
How went your study in the morning class?

THYESTES: Boring! The man's an ass...

ATREUS: *(giggles to himself)* ... Without the attributes.

THYESTES: *(Mimicking the tutor. talking slowly, rhythmically and breathlessly.)*
'He talks/ as if/ each breath/ will be/ his last.

ATREUS: Mama, must we learn these ancient laws?
They're dry as dirt, and dull as proclamations 'bout the war.

HIPPODAMIA: You must do well!
Good rulers know how all the laws were formed,
And which ones they can break, and which uphold.
You must do well! What subject have you next?

ATREUS: Poetry! With Strabo,
Prancing round, reciting boring verse!

HIPPODAMIA: No! No! Even that, learn well.
The greater range of subjects you control,
The greater is your power to rule and reign.

ATREUS: But mama, he's so effete!

THYESTES: He even makes young Chrysippus look bold.

(Enter Livia)

LIVIA: Your majesty, Lucien has returned.

41

HIPPODAMIA: Lucien!
Then show him in, I'm waiting on this news.

ATREUS: Oh mama,
Do we have to study poetry, to rule,
Can't we stay and listen to your news?

HIPPODAMIA: No. Off you go.
All knowledge has a value and a place,
Learn well my chicks, one day you'll see the sense.

(The boys exit)

(Lucien, looking very dishevelled enters, slowly.)

Oh Lucien, you're safe!
My heart has been a whirlpool since you left,
Not knowing if you lived or if you died.
Here, let me hold you in my arms...
Your Hands! Your Clothes! Why so rudely clad?

LUCIEN: Your majesty.
The soldiers from King Laius' camp, abused me.
Beating me and rolling me in filth.

HIPPODAMIA: No!

LUCIEN: I was imprisoned in a rat-infested den,
And starved of food and water overnight,
With nowhere but the earth to lay my head.

HIPPODAMIA: Oh my poor and loyal servant. Such abuse!
I'll have revenge!
No man of mine shall be so vilely treated by those scum.
I'll find these ragged fiends who did you harm
And disembowel each one of them in turn
Until their bleeding entrails fill his court
And blood becomes more common there than air.
Did he then refuse my chance of peace?

LUCIEN: He took the news most strangely I observed.
At first, he raged, as though in mortal pain,
And then he fell upon me, like a priest,
Suspicious of my purpose and my task.
He grabbed my gentle windpipe with his hands

42

And squeezed his grip upon it like a vice,
Until I thought I'd choked and gasped my last.
Whereat, he clawed and slashed me with his nails,
Like some demented animal gone wild,
And frothing at the mouth, with rabies foam.

HIPPODAMIA: Vile beast! My poor, gentle Lucien. What then?

LUCIEN: I fought him off.

HIPPODAMIA: Most brave.

LUCIEN: But all his mighty army stood around,
And held me down while he pursued his fit,
And then, at last, he wandered some way off
To hold a conversation with the air.

HIPPODAMIA: The air?
Good! Good! They say his mind is fraught with haunted
dreams.
This serves my purpose well.
What next? What next? Tell on.

LUCIEN: Why, then he seemed to change. Surveyed the field;
Addressed his men, and had me led away,
To all that rough confine I spoke before.

HIPPODAMIA: And then?

LUCIEN: Then morning came, and I awoke in pain,
Not knowing if I'd see the whole day through
Or if my life was doomed to perish there.
Then heard I strange commotion in the court;
Laius, wailing and weeping, like a raging bull,
And soldiers running, like an army had invaded overnight.
All this I heard from in my dark confine,
My hands and limbs still bleeding from their wounds.

HIPPODAMIA: Indignity beyond belief!
These fiends shall taste the wrath of my revenge.

LUCIEN: At length,
Long after midday sun had reached its height,
He sent for me, and bade me here return,
Agreeing to your meeting him tonight.

43

HIPPODAMIA: Tonight! That is not what I said!

LUCIEN: You said that you would meet him in the dark
             The place reserved, the time the bridge of night.
             He said,
             "Your thus appointed place, we there shall meet.
             The hour we'll split, that it may suit us both,
             Your midnight, and my tonight."
             And then I was ejected from the court.

HIPPODAMIA: Tonight! Tonight! It goes against my plans.
             The moon is full tonight,
             And I have here some business in the court.
             Yet, let it come on.
             His speed may yet betray his weakest point.

LUCIEN: Have I done well?

HIPPODAMIA: Oh Lucien, your bravery would shame our bravest men,
             And all your hardships suffered for my cause,
             Will be rewarded with a full, and gentle love.
             Go. Tend your wounds and sleep a worthy sleep,
             My pleasure will reward you by and by.

             (exit Lucien)

             Tonight....
             Now comes on my plan, with greater speed
             Than ever I could hope.

             (enter the Watchman.)

WATCHMAN:*(to himself)* Ghaarrr! *(slowly)* Your ma-jes-ty.

HIPPODAMIA: You!
             What brings you crawling here, you vermin'd scum?

WATCHMAN: I was not always painted so.
             You did not mock me when I eased your cruel distress.
             I still provide a service, should you wish.

HIPPODAMIA: Speak! Then Go!
             I shall not waste more breath on your account.

WATCHMAN: Lucien has returned.

44

HIPPODAMIA: I know! You imbecilic cur!
Is this your news? The total value of your hobbled word?
Some watchman you've become!
Relaying warnings when the Action's done!

WATCHMAN: Even a mangy mongrel lifts its leg,
Before it licks its master's eager face.
That was not my news, but merely observation of events.

HIPPODAMIA: You dare to mock me?

WATCHMAN: I? I would not mock the hand that feeds me!
No. Not I.
I merely utter, what my watchful eyes perceive.

HIPPODAMIA: Your news and make it brief.
My temper runs upon its o'er spurred heights,
And longs to fall full gallop at your throat.

WATCHMAN: Neigh! You do not wish to harm me.

HIPPODAMIA: Harm you!
I'll flay each inch of flesh from off your bones.
Your news and make it quick.
(She raises her hand as if to strike him. - he ducks.)

WATCHMAN: Oedipus! Oedipus! My news concerns young Oedipus,
Who's due to make a Captain here tonight.

HIPPODAMIA: Go on.

WATCHMAN: Lately, in our camp, which stinks of sweating men,
Some rabble scum from Corinth have arrived,
To help us in this war against Old Thebes.
Black ugly brutes, but then you like them dark...

HIPPODAMIA: On!

WATCHMAN: They set to drinking when the battle stops
And drink until their bladder's fit to burst,
Then piss their stinking urine where they will.

HIPPODAMIA: *(she slaps him.)*
Come to the point, you foul-mouthed, twisted, wart!

WATCHMAN: Ghaarrr!

45

One of their horde, a burly, bearded tyke,
Who pisses more than most with half his length,
Is new returned from visiting his home.
While there, in Corinth, Mastering his wife, *(he mimics this)*
He's called before the King to give account,
Of how their prince, young Oedipus, has fared.
This soldier tells his tale with swollen chest,
Young Oedipus has proved himself a man
- Not only in the camp among the whores -
But also on the field against real men:
Poking and thrusting, jabbing, stabbing home! *(he mimics this)*
King Polybus is close to pissing tears:
"My son! My Son!", he cries,
"What father's joy! What sheer delight he brings!"
Then, the old fool, cuckolded by his fears,
Breaks down and weeps:
"Oh would that such a child had been my son!
Oh would that I had spawned such vital youth,
Not found him as a babe on Cithaeron's hill."
The court grows silent in its disbelief.
The King comes to, denying all he's said,
And charged - on pain of death - all lips be sealed.
And so it was, 'till early yester' night,
When our fat tyke, now full and lacking sense,
Through swilling down, too much grape-juice sperm,
Blurts his secret out, and pisses in the wind,
This dreadful bugbear of old Corinth's King.

HIPPODAMIA: So Oedipus is not the rightful heir!

WATCHMAN: Squeeze on your thighs, don't wet your knickers yet!
The best is yet to come.
The word spins round the camp,
That Oedipus is not his father's son.
A royal bastard, from some bastard's womb!
At length this poxy tale, enlarged with every telling,
Like the rod, that's swollen by the pox it passes on,
Kisses our young hero on his ear,
And licks its poison deep into his brain.

HIPPODAMIA: How did the news affect him when he heard?

WATCHMAN: Across the camp he ran,
Like someone held his woman in their arms,
And in one swipe,
Had severed all the parts, that make a man,

From off that burbling, blabber-mouthing fool!
The rumours stop! All ears forget their sound!
And no one dare suggest he's not well-born.
Oedipus, son of Polybus, King of Corinth!
Ha! Ha! Ha! Ha!

HIPPODAMIA: Your vile tale, made fouler in the telling by your tongue,
Does not displease.
Where is he now, this unknown-father's son?

WATCHMAN: He's coming here to claim his rightful due;
A Captaincy, and ribbon in our ranks.

HIPPODAMIA: Good!
Get you back to camp, you've served me well.
Here, take these, you're due some small reward.
(she gives him some coins.)

WATCHMAN: Dry coins? *(he spits on them)*
I'd rather, like your Lucien, get a wet reward.
(she slaps him)
Ghaarrr! I'll buy one then.

(He limps off.)

HIPPODAMIA: No better news my ears could want to hear.
Oedipus, no son to Polybus. Ha!

(Chrysippus enters, sees Hippodamia and draws back into hiding to observe her)

This knowledge will do well to cause a rift
Between this upstart youth and his dear friend.
I'll give some thought to this divise anon.

(Exit Hippodamia.)

CHRYSIPPUS: What evil scheme absorbs her thinking now?
See, how eagerly she goes,
The silent cat, to spring upon her foes.
But hold,
That was a thought unworthy to express.
Why does she gall me so, and turn my thoughts to hate?
Oh Oedipus, I would that you were here,
I long to hold you, feel your strength once more,
Engage in disputations as before!

47

I need your comfort and your friendly warmth,
To give me courage 'gainst these 'loving' foes,
Who feign close friendship, while they act with hate,
And make me feel a stranger in my home,
Where every day that woman gains in power.
And yet, I know that gentleness and love,
Must triumph o'er the most insidious foe,
'Else we remain no better than the beasts.
(Music begins to play - off.)
Ha!
They start rehearsing for your royal feast,
And still you are not here. Oh Oedipus,
I would you were on time for this salute.
My father does you honour with this act
But little knows you care not for such praise,
For you and I deplore such worldly rank
Preferring humble wisdom to this pomp.
Poor father, befuddled in your love!
Your mind is clouded by that woman's art
And led in chains down truth-denying tracks
Where she embroils you with her silken lies.
Oh Father!
Do I see clearly that her so-called love,
Is but a means of holding you in thrall,
Or does my mother's death - as you have claimed -
Cast shadows o'er the way that I perceive?
Oh Oedipus, I would that you were here,
To give some sanction to these sordid thoughts,
Or castigate my mind for breeding lies!
That woman boils my blood with every breath,
And turns to anger all my gentle thoughts,
Transforming and transmuting them to hate,
Against my best attempts to give her love.
She would derange my senses if she could,
And agitate my mind till it runs wild,
And screams its hollow madness to the wind.
I do not hate her, yet she loves me not,
And seems so full of anger at my being,
That were I not my father's only son
I fear she would have ended me by now.
She is a serpent with a venomed tongue,
Who works like canker on the silent rose,
Her vicious words - designed to mar and maim -
Like poison slowly seep into the brain
Polluting and discolouring one's thought
Until, at last, her rot fills every pore,

48

Subjecting one completely to her power.
And thus she wraps my father in her spell,
Confining him within a self-spun hell;
The one part made by his too restless thought
The other fed with her pernicious lies.
Poor father, what a curse this love has brought,
Embroiling you within its gungy web
And spreading suff'ring like a raging plague.
All this I know is true beyond debate,
And witness daily with unbiased eyes.
Yet who believes a youth who worships Truth,
And dreams of worlds where men can live in peace?

(Enter Oedipus unseen.)

Yet time will prove true judge of all her art,
For those, who moral are, are well reborn,
While those who evil use, are evilly disposed -
Or so those Eastern sages thus maintain.

(Oedipus comes forward.)

OEDIPUS: Sweet Chrysippus,
              What heavy thoughts now weigh your spirits down?
              Here, let me comfort you awhile.

(Chrysippus runs to him. they embrace.)

CHRYSIPPUS: Oh Oedipus, you've come at last.
              My heart had lost all hope of your return.

OEDIPUS: And so you waste your time in idle thought,
              Questioning the meaning of this world.

(They part)

CHRYSIPPUS: Oh no! Not idle. You know as well as I,
              Our lives are governed by some unseen laws
              Which I would have discovered and made known.
              I wrestle with myself in this debate,
              And seek to make some sense of what I see.
              I need your help to set my mind aright,
              And guide me to the truth of all these thoughts.
              Our eyes play tricks, and oft'times foul our sight.
              Can we believe what happens to us here,
              When memory may later feed us lies?...

49

OEDIPUS: Do not talk thus!
              You live in dreams! In lands of make believe!
              Do not destroy your life in such pursuits,
              What use is thought like that, to men who fight?

CHRYSIPPUS: Use? Use? It has no use!
              You cannot value thought!
              It gives some reason to the lives we lead;
              Some purpose to the actions we pursue,
              Some meaning to the mysteries of life.
              If we deny ourselves the use of thought
              Our time on earth is no more than a dream
              - A veiled illusion of some grander scheme -
              Where blind and senseless, reeling in dismay,
              We blunder from one hardship to the next,
              With no control o'er what we do or say.
              Without clear thought, we are but helpless sheep,
              Who run in herds for comfort and for strength,
              And 'baa' together like the braying mob.

OEDIPUS: These are just childish fantasies and whims.
              The comforts here in court have made you soft!
              You're raving like a madman, crazed with shock!

CHRYSIPPUS: No! No!
              I seek for Truth. It means so much to me -
              And lately held a value for you too.
              How have you changed?
              Have you forgot so soon our constant talk,
              Our plans of how we'd make a perfect world?
              Those nights we spent in discourse long and fierce,
              Arguing the subtleties of thought,
              Which shone and glittered through our eager minds,
              'Till creeping Dawn awoke the dozing skies,
              And draped her sun-kissed mantle 'cross our eyes,
              Which, drawing on, enlightened every thought,
              Until we leapt the confines of this earth
              To course great tracts of space, imagined free.
              For hours on hours our words created worlds,
              'Till Sleep Herself, took Reason from our tongues,
              And bathed our o'er fired heads in soothing dreams.
              Recall you nothing of this happy past?

OEDIPUS: That was before, when I was yet a child,
              But now I am a man and think with this.

(he brandishes his sword.)
These idle thoughts we prattled in our youth
Soon vanish in the face of demon Death.
I know but little of the Thinker's art,
Being more akin to action and to war.

CHRYSIPPUS: But all your actions make you what you are!
You need not violence to attain your ends.
We've dreamt of how the world should truly be.
How love and kindness, soothe all wars away.

OEDIPUS: Be that as it may.
I did not come to argue points of view,
But share a rare companionship with you,
And feel your boyish innocence and youth.
(He holds his face in his hands)
But do you feed me with the love I need?
No!
You fill my ears with this unwholesome whine
Like some ungrateful whore who screams for more
And casts me from her bed like some cheap slave!
Is this the welcome that a friend deserves?

CHRYSIPPUS: Oh Oedipus, forgive my lack of thought,
Your welcome here is more than words can say.
I've waited for your friendship for so long
I know not how to make my feelings show.

(They embrace again)

So many nights I've longed to hold you near,
And feel the comfort of your beating heart,
Engage in wild discussions as before.
But yet, your view of life has somehow, changed.
I cannot understand.
Do you now, no longer seek for Truth?
So many hours together have we spent
Enwrapt in Disputation's fiery robe.
Does She, no longer fill your mind with joy,
Or light those fires which burn with Wisdom's flame?

OEDIPUS: Chrysippus!
I am a soldier in your father's ranks,
A Captain, if my purpose here be known,
That, is what ignites my mind with joy:
That is where your pyres of Wisdom burn.

51

My arm is strong; my sword, sharp-whetted steel,
That cuts all false imaginings in two.
'Tis man 'gainst man, that's what this life's about,
And climbing through the ranks to reach the top.

CHRYSIPPUS: Oh Oedipus! This tone befits you not!

OEDIPUS: This tone is what I am!
               The cry of battle and the smell of blood,
               That's what my life's become!
               In yonder field lies all you need to know
               'Bout life and death, and love, and joy, and war.
               I am myself and strive to my own ends.
               I am a hero in the public's eye.
               In time, I'll rule a kingdom, be a king
               Controlling armies with a single word!
               Taste you not the taste of Truth in this?

CHRYSIPPUS: Oh Oedipus, I know not what to say....
               Since last we met your view of life has changed.
               I little knew how quickly men could change.
               That Alteration's hand was so adept;
               Indoctrination's method so complete.
               (And yet my father proves this through his love.)
               But six short months... can this be so?
               To throw away the vision we admired:
               Of men in peace together; mutual love;
               Of gentleness, of ...

OEDIPUS: Six months! Six years! What matters what the time?
               The smell of armies and the cries of men,
               That's where my life belongs!
               When I was younger,
               In my father's court in Corinth, I, like you,
               Being virginal, and innocent of life,
               Dreamt dreams, made schemes, and conjured up to view,
               Vast visions of the perfect state of man.
               So, when we met - some countless months before -
               Our minds inflamed each other with our views.
               But now, I've tasted life. I am a man!
               And see the world through eyes that are mature,
               While you - cocooned as yet - within this court,
               Know little of the workings of the world,
               Or any of the tastes or joys of war.
               Listen, while I tell what does befall,
               And picture my existence in our camp,

Where life is cheap and careless, rude and raw,
Where one does all one's living, in Death's jaw!
Envisage here a battle on a plain;
Two armies poised, arrayed in serried ranks,
Each staring at the other glazed with hate,
And eager for the order to attack.
Anticipation's silence shakes the air,
And carries on the wind the smell of fear.
While short of breath, the jostling swordsmen gasp,
To add their seething anger to this mass.
Then, down the line, a signal from afar,
Flashes like a flame, from sword to sword.
Our Captains raise their banners, and we charge,
To greet our hapless foe with bloody death!
Sharp metals clash, wild cries torment the air,
And heavy blows rain down like spring-tide's flood
Till all around men sink into that mud,
And turn the ground to crimson with their blood.
A bugle brays, we pause to take account,
Regrouping on a hill to toll our dead,
And curse the swine who decimate our ranks.
We start a chant, a roaring with our tongues,
Which fills the air with all its horrid sound.
As wild mosquitoes' buzzing, stings the ear
Before its sharp proboscis stings the flesh,
So shouting boys, and banging drummers' drums,
Stirs up the fear of death in all our foes,
Before our blood-wet swords strike home their blows.
We wait.
Each heart-beat pumping hate around our veins
Until at last the order comes. We're off!
Our swords upraised and bright against the sun,
Running like a demon through their ranks.
They break; we fight and chase them further back!
More shouts. More steel on steel resounds.
A cry! A gasp! A fallen soldier drowns.
We run. Push on, strike harder 'gainst our foe.
Until each sword reeks death with every blow.
At last their spirits crumble and they break,
And with one voice they turn their backs and run
A pack of wild and screaming, frenzied, men,
Arrayed across this battlefield like wraiths.
We give them chase,
And slay each lilied coward as he runs,
'Till not one single man is left alive!
We've won! The victory is ours!

Our standard's flying boldly in the sun,
We've Won! Won! Rejoice! The Victory is ours!
Sound up the bugles! Split the joyous air!
Scream our army's triumph to the skies,
And feel those Victor's tears, stream from your eyes!
There! That's delight! That's living at the full!
No whore-rich bed e'er gave my flesh such joy!
No thinking, ever spun my giddy brain,
No exaltation ever filled my veins.
'Till I, in battle, felt the Victor's gains!
And in that moment life and death are one,
Triumphant with a power no tongue can speak.
'Tis then we reach the goal your mystics seek,
And vindicate all searching after truth!
There! That's what Life's about!
These visions that you have of good and bad,
Of Life being made by mankind's love of man,
Live to breathe their last in Death's vast tomb,
For men engender Life in War's dark Womb!
Chrysippus! Why start you so, your face is pale,
Your visage like a ghost?

CHRYSIPPUS: I see a ghost! A former friend, now dead,
Fills these eyes with terror and with fright.
Can wasteful war so change a man's intents
To blind him from himself and all his good?

OEDIPUS: Come! Shake out of this! There's no ghost here!
Your eyes do but play mischief with your brain.

CHRYSIPPUS: Oh yes. There is a ghost indeed!
A former self now stranded here on earth,
To walk forever through this barren waste,
And never see the light of sunlit day,
Nor turn its face to Beauty's soothing sight.
Your actions have condemned you to this fate,
While all this senseless killing, kills your sense!

OEDIPUS: Do not talk thus!
War is at the core of every man!
My story of the battle's made you quake,
This talk of ghosts but shows your woman's fear!

CHRYSIPPUS: AM I AN ISLAND IN THIS SEA OF PAIN?
Have you no eyes to see what you have done?
Felt you no compassion for the foe,

54

No grain of human feeling for his woe;
His pain and sorrow, anguish and defeat?
Is he not human too and cries like us,
Has loved ones left at home to mourn his loss?
Has mother, father, sister, brother, friend;
Who on his love, for nourishment depend?
Does he not leave some happy bed unfilled;
Some tiny hand denied its father's grasp;
Some hungry mouth, now greater fast to bear;
Some faithful wife bequeathed, but more, despair?
And you exalt this carnage as Life's Goal?
These precious bonds built up through pain and strife,
By layer on layer of hard-won love and trust,
Into some faint and shimmering ray of hope,
Destroyed by you in one despotic thrust,
To gratify your own pathetic lust!

OEDIPUS: Chrysippus!
(Lays his hand on Chrysippus's arm).

CHRYSIPPUS: Unhand me! Bloody butcher of men's flesh!
Do not taint me with your unholy guilt!
I'd rather face this life alone, in pain,
Than share the smallest drop of it with you!

(Exit Chrysippus)

OEDIPUS: Chrysippus! Come back!
This loud bravado is but surface deep,
To hide my finer feelings from the mob.
(pause)
Reviled and rightly so. Oh bloody hands,
That ever you were eager for men's death,
Rip out this pipe which binds me to the earth.
Chrysippus, come back,
You little guess the depth of pain I feel.
I seem a butcher to your tender eyes,
Yet since I took up arms, my whole World's war!
My life: an endless battle 'gainst my foes -
Not men, arrayed against me with their swords -
But thoughts and feelings, arguments and words,
Whose deaf'ning clamour rises in one voice,
To scream dissatisfaction with my life!
And now,
To crush forever all my hopes and joys,
This latest pain, brought freshly from my home,

- Where love and comfort ever should reside -
Ungrateful questions 'bout my parentage and line,
That mark me as a bastard whoreson dog!
Must I be cursed forever for this fault,
Sought out and mocked for actions not my own?
I'd rather gouge these eyes from out this head,
Than see my fate rejoiced in gloating looks,
By those whose weaker spirits suffer not!
(He falls to his knees weeping)
Oh Chrysippus,
My heart is bleeding from the want of love!
I need some human kindness to survive.
Help me!

(Enter a spirit likeness of Chrysippus, bathed in golden light - unseen by Oedipus)

How glassy strange this world now wetly looks.
These tear-strained eyes distort the sights they view,
And give to simple objects, magic powers.
My vision seems encased in glowing light,
As if some misty stillness trapped all sight,
And focussed it upon some unknown realm.
What can this be?
What dreamy state cocoons me in its arms?
My skin begins to glow with warm delight,
As if my blood was nectar from the gods,
Pulsing with the vibrancy of Life!
Oh joy unbounded!
And feel my breath, how rhythmic it becomes,
While all the air smells perfumed, fresh and clear,
As if this room no longer was confined,
But opened up to space on every side.
What harmonies this silence seems to hold.
Soft music, plays and dances, in my ear,
And ripples out its tune with such sweet ease,
It fills me with a rapture, rich and rare.
What blissful realm is this?
What death foreboding state have I attained?
Is this some glimpse of heav'n before I die?
What's this?
What phantom shade now stalks me from my dreams?
Some form that has no form yet keeps a shape.
I do not fear it, yet I quake in fright.
It glows yet seems translucent in this light.
Chrysippus! Tis he. And yet tis not.

Some spirit body that assumes his form.
Is't he, or is it not?
It moves! Hold! Hold, I say.
Stand still awhile you creature of delight
That I may bathe these pupils in your sight.
How moving. How refined.
It glows like burnished gold in flame's red light.
Exudes sweet gentle rays of soothing calm,
As if its very essence is pure Love.
What ecstasies this image does incite!
Gold honied-warmth flows o'er me like a balm,
That bathes my tired flesh in fresh delights.
My mind is calm. My senses all acute.
My vision bright and full as ne'er before.
I feel like some old god - empowered anew!
Sweet Chrysippus, is this how you appear,
Are you this heavenly creature I behold;
The answer to my prayers, and all my woe?
Wait! Don't go! I will not do you harm.
Wait! Why shy away? I seek to give you love.
Do not desert me in my hour of need.

(He is about to exit after the spirit when Hippodamia enters.)

HIPPODAMIA: Ah! Oedipus, I would a word with you.

OEDIPUS: *(aside)* It fades as if some blackness dulled its light.

HIPPODAMIA: Oedipus!

OEDIPUS: *(aside)*These god-like feelings drain as it departs.
Don't go. I would enjoy your company awhile.

HIPPODAMIA: Oedipus. Attend me.

OEDIPUS: Oh, your majesty. I did not hear you call.
See you not this form?

HIPPODAMIA: What childish jest is this? I see you well enough.

OEDIPUS: No. Not I. This other form.
So fair. So kind. So gentle in its ways.

HIPPODAMIA: What foolishness is this? Desist!
We are alone. There are no others here.
I have not time to play these childish games.

OEDIPUS: (*aside*) Don't go!
                  Your comfort's draining as your brightness fades.
                  (*aloud*) You see no other form?

HIPPODAMIA: Nothing!
                  Your mind's o'er heated from the battle's fray.
                  Attend. I have some thoughts we must review,
                  Regarding your position in our court.

OEDIPUS: (*aside*)She does not see? Yet it seems real to me.

HIPPODAMIA: Oedipus!

OEDIPUS: Your majesty.
                  I would some other moment would befit,
                  My mind is in a turmoil at this time.

HIPPODAMIA: I'll not delay you long.
                  I think our topic will afford you joy,
                  And bring some comfort to your o'er wrought brain,
                  Which seems in need of some such soothing balm.

OEDIPUS: (*aside*) No balm could equal this.
                  (*To the vision*) Stay! I beg you not to leave.

HIPPODAMIA: Pay heed.
                  What do you gaze at? Fix your eyes on me.
                  Oedipus!

OEDIPUS: Madame.
                  (*He looks longingly after the fading figure.*)
                  (*aside*) Oh no. It goes.
                  My spirit slumps once more to human realms.

HIPPODAMIA: Oedipus. What say you? Don't discourse with yourself.
                  Shake off this drowsy slumber. Pay me heed.
                  I'm here for your own good.

OEDIPUS: (*aside*) It's shadow seemed to tremble at these words.
                  Tis gone. And comfort at its heels.
                  I am alone.

HIPPODAMIA: Oedipus. Shake off this mood. Attend.
                  Tonight, before the king and all his court,
                  You will be raised to Captain in our ranks

58

An honour not bestowed on every man...

OEDIPUS: (*hangs his head*)
               I now begin to doubt that I am fit,
               To take what once I saw as my due right.
               Such rank and power seem worthless to me now.
               I feel ashamed of ever seeking praise.

HIPPODAMIA: Lift up your head. You have no shame to bear.
               You are a hero in our country's eyes,
               Despite...

OEDIPUS: Despite?

HIPPODAMIA: Oh...
               There is some garbled rumour from the camp.

OEDIPUS: Rumour? What rumour?

HIPPODAMIA: Oh a trifle. Some gossip 'mongst the troops.
               Some idle jest. Not worthy to repeat.

OEDIPUS: What idle jest?

HIPPODAMIA: Oedipus! Do not disturb yourself.
               I do not give my ear to common talk.

OEDIPUS: And yet you hear it.
               Tell me what you've heard,
               If gossip reaches you from my command,
               I'll rip the liar's tongue from out his throat!

HIPPODAMIA: Do not distress yourself!
               The matter's so absurd it slips my mind.

OEDIPUS: Then I will catch it 'fore it slips too far!
               (*He shakes her violently*)

HIPPODAMIA: Unhand me brute! You do forget your place!

OEDIPUS: Your majesty. Forgive me. (*he kneels*)
               I am distressed and know not what I do.
               My temper rides so finely in its scales,
               One simple word can plunge it into rage.
               (*He turns to where the figure was*)
               (*aside*) How quickly have I fall'n from that pure height.

(*He turns back*)
(*aloud*) Oh! Your majesty.
Can you forgive such outrage 'gainst yourself?

HIPPODAMIA: Arise dear boy, I'm not a cripple yet.
Your fury got the better of your sense.
Here, take my hand.
This hurt must be severe to cause such pain.
Come, my bosom's soft, unburden here your grief.

OEDIPUS: Oh! My mind is like a stallion wild with rage,
That charges at our foes with blinkered eyes,
Not knowing where its course will fin'lly lead.
I am a man, a soldier by my trade,
But since I've plied these skills, my life has changed.
Unhappiness has grown with each new death,
As if the men I've killed were part of me,
And killing them, kills off my finer self.
Some moments, hence, I floated in a dream,
And tasted peace-and-quiet quite unknown.
Some apparition from a godly realm
Fed me with the fruits of His estate,
And stilled this sense of dying for a while.
Now it is gone. And with it goes my heart
For Chrysippus, my gentle, loving, friend,
Whose very form this apparition chose,
Has joined the ranks of those who turn their backs,
And slander my endeavour with their lies,
Claiming that I live for death alone!

HIPPODAMIA: Then they are fools. And he's the biggest fool.

OEDIPUS: 'Tis his displeasure smarts my heart the most,
And salts my wounds by echoing of truth.
I long to find some comfort in his arms,
And end this ceaseless conflict with my self.
(*aside*) Oh vap'rous creature visit me once more,
Release me from the confines of this Hell!

HIPPODAMIA: Control yourself!
These tender feelings rob you of your power.
Your mind is quite unbalanced by this youth.
There are no apparitions in this court
- 'cept Chrysippus himself -
And he's a fickle child who's giv'n to fits,
And thinks himself far grander than he is.

Do not distress yourself on his account.
Come, leave well alone. Pay heed to me.
I'm here to help you ease this heavy load.
Come. Tell me of this wound which cuts so deep?
What is this pain? What are these hurtful lies?
What is this rumour that assails our ranks?

OEDIPUS: You've heard the gossip and must know it well.

HIPPODAMIA: Not I. I little heed the gossiping of fools,
But would be keen to hear this tale from you,
Your strength and valour, manliness, and youth,
Will guarantee the truth of what you tell.

OEDIPUS: But what is truth? This is half my pain.
Oh! Chrysippus would lash me with his tongue,
If ever he should learn of this misdeed:
To lose my temper over gossips' tongues,
And take a life defending drunken jests.
I should be cast a madman, not a Prince!

HIPPODAMIA: That Chrysippus is wise before his time,
His venomed tongue makes poison of his speech!
Heed not his sense of truth.
Come.
In simple words relate your tale to me,
I'm sure we two, can judge what's true, or false.

OEDIPUS: Oh Chrysippus,
What fires are raging in this aching heart?
Relieve me with your love.
(The spirit likeness appears again.)
(aside) It comes again.

HIPPODAMIA: Forget that boy. Relate your tale to me.
This worship of his youth becomes you not,
Such feelings are effeminate in men.

OEDIPUS: I love him. Yet I still remain a man.

HIPPODAMIA: Do women not attract you more than boys?
I am a woman, and your trust should flow to me,
Not hover round the whims of wimpish youths.

OEDIPUS: *(aside)* Don't go.

HIPPODAMIA: Attend me boy. Where is your manhood now?
Where all your valour from the battle's fray?

OEDIPUS: My valour seems mere folly to me now.
I'm torn in two, by forces I know not.

HIPPODAMIA: Shake out of this. I'll show you where you lie.
(She grabs him roughly and kisses him on the lips)
There! Know where you belong.

(The spirit departs - defeated.)

OEDIPUS: Your majesty!

HIPPODAMIA: Look not so shocked. I am a woman too.
Think you Pelops satisfies my needs?
Come. Recount your tale.
My favours may well serve as your reward.

OEDIPUS: I never saw your majesty before.

HIPPODAMIA: But I've seen you.
(She kisses him again - lightly)
Now. Quickly. To your tale. Before we are disturbed.
We must relieve your suffering at once.

OEDIPUS: I never guessed you felt this way before.

HIPPODAMIA: I cannot always show what's in my heart,
For fear that my advances will be spurned.

OEDIPUS: Oh no! I will not be untrue.
But hope to prove the equal to your love.

HIPPODAMIA: Then prove it now, by telling me your tale.
Ease your sorrow. Share with me this pain,
And help our mutual feelings to unfold.

OEDIPUS: Oh what a source of comfort does this bring,
To know that I may share this pain with you,
And trust that your true love will guide me through.
T'was like a dream, and only yesternight...
Some fellow kinsmen, new returned from home,
Were shaking off the battle from their limbs,
By filling up their minds with drink's delights,
And telling tales from Corinth's distant court.

When, one fat ugly brute - more drunk than most -
Roars out abuse that pained me to the heart.

HIPPODAMIA: What could he shout to ruffle such as you?

OEDIPUS: This ugly brute spread rumours round the camp,
Pertaining to the nature of my birth,
By making out I'm not my father's son!

HIPPODAMIA: Strong words from servile tongues!
Did you not contest this sland'rous talk?

OEDIPUS: Contest?
I buried it, along with his thick skull.

HIPPODAMIA: Brave boy! Your actions suit your thoughts.
Howe'er, perhaps you were too rash,
For now we'll never know quite what he meant.
Unless...

OEDIPUS: Unless?

HIPPODAMIA: Oh, a fleeting thought.

OEDIPUS: Tell all!
Do not keep secret any of your thoughts.

HIPPODAMIA: Be not distressed. My thought is simple.
And may well prove as simple as that brute.
He may have meant no harm by his remark,
But spoke it to enhance your father's charm.
What shame is there to know that in his youth,
Your father was an active, virile, man?

OEDIPUS: There's shame enough for me!
To think my mother was a cheap camp whore,
Devours my self respect.
How can I order men who mock me thus?
And, if my mother justifies that name,
What father spawned me? Wherein lies his fame?

HIPPODAMIA: I know your father, and his wealthy lands,
And in his youth, he was a man of... joy.
Why all the world is guilty of his crime.
I hold no doubts that you're his rightful son,
(Your valour and your bearing mark you so).

63

But this is no disgrace, a man's a man,
A king's a king, and you are still a prince,
Although your loving mother may not be,
The same as she who is the present queen.

OEDIPUS: Then which one gave the lie?
You claim my father is my sire, while others claim
My mother's in the right.
I'll never know for sure which tale is true
For both will stick together in their lie,
Maintaining 'gainst all odds that I am pure,
For if I'm not, our lineage must cease,
And pass to distant cousins of our line.

HIPPODAMIA: Do not despair! Your torment can be eased.
You can, with some small, effort learn the truth.

OEDIPUS: How? What?

HIPPODAMIA: In Delphi, at Apollo's mighty shrine,
The Oracle of Knowledge holds His court.
Go there.
Give voice to all these doubts which wear you down.
He'll make pronouncement, no man dare to fault,
And guarantee your right to wear that crown.

OEDIPUS: Delphi! Apollo's shrine! Why yes,
He'll know the Truth. The answer that I seek.
Why did this not occur to me before?
'Tis some days hence. I'll catch the morning tide,
After I've discharged my business here.

HIPPODAMIA: No! Go at once!
I'll reason forth your absence from the court.

OEDIPUS: My Captaincy, I must attend for that.
King Pelops does me honour with this gift,
I cannot throw such kindness in his face
- e'en thought I doubt my worth for such a prize.

HIPPODAMIA: Your Captaincy can wait.

OEDIPUS: But why?
This storm can blow no worse in one short night.

HIPPODAMIA: Pelops is a man with strange designs,

And should he ever hear - from some sour tongue -
That something was amiss with your descent,
Would have you banished rudely from the court.

OEDIPUS: Pelops? He does not strike me so!
He is a man whom Fairness seems to favour with Her role.
I never found him partisan or bent,
To give more ear to one cause than the rest.

HIPPODAMIA: I am his wife and know him more than you.
There's many a man in public seems a god,
Who in his private life's no more than beast.
He suffers from a strange and sad complaint,
'bout cleanliness and matters of descent.
Why, did I not with scrupulous concern,
Spell out my royal lineage to him,
Before he even deigned to hear my pleas
That love for him consumed my burning heart.
Why, only after hours of penance done
Would he consider marriage as a thought,
And even then, was loathful to agree,
'till further gods, with further gifts, were bought.

OEDIPUS: I did not know he held religion so!

HIPPODAMIA: Forget his follies now, 'tis you our thoughts are with.
Your needs must have some comfort from this pain,
So go at once,
For Delphi is the only balm I know.

OEDIPUS: Sweet balm indeed.
I long to pluck this thorn from out my heart,
Wherein it hourly festers like a sore,
That fills my fevered brain with rancid pus!
And yet,
To leave without farewell seems - somehow - wrong.
And Chrysippus, I must regain his love.
He left distraught that I had killed and maimed,
And felt no true compassion for my foe...

HIPPODAMIA: His childish brain is yet unknown to Life,
O'er pampered by the comforts of our court.
Attend to your own needs and leave at once.
Forget his whims, he wastes his life in dreams.

OEDIPUS: E'en so,

The sound of truth rings through his simple words,
And causes me much questioning and doubt.
I needs must comfort him. And show him that I care.
Our friendship was in ruins when he left.

HIPPODAMIA: No! Go at once!
My pleas to you are made from selfish love.
If Pelops hears, before you know the truth,
You may be barred forever from our lands,
And never plumb the depth of my full heart.
Pay heed to what I say, for both our sakes.

OEDIPUS: Oh! Such total kindness from an unsuspected friend.
I would we could explore our friendship now,
And I, at least, repay your selfless love.

HIPPODAMIA: No. There's time enough. Let's see your future safe,
Before we think to further our own ends.
The blossom picked too soon will fade and die,
Before its fruit has swollen and shed its seed.
This parting can be seen as one more test,
To prove our mutual love is strong and true.

OEDIPUS: My heart is torn in two.

HIPPODAMIA: Go! Relieve your heart.
I'll pacify all parties left behind,
And plead your case with such a fervent voice,
That they'll chastise the sweetness of my tongue,
For holding your departure for so long.

OEDIPUS: Oh! I do not know.

HIPPODAMIA: Then go!
Inaction makes the nest where sloth will grow.
Do this deed now, and clear your troubled mind,
Then claim your rightful honour, with fresh pride.

OEDIPUS: I'll go.
And you'll aright all matters here in court?

HIPPODAMIA: Done! Done! A hundred times done!

OEDIPUS: And Chrysippus, what of my love for him?

HIPPODAMIA: I will take pains to see that he's informed,

Of all the salient reasons for your flight.
He would be first to urge you to this course.
Now go at once, and catch the turning tide,
Before it leaves the harbour stale and flat.
The sooner you approach that holy shrine
The sooner will your anguish be removed.
Come! I'll speed you on your way.

(Exit Oedipus and Hippodamia).

END OF ACT 1 SCENE 5

ACT 1 SCENE 6

A barren rock-strewn track high in the mountains. windswept, cold and desolate. Enter the boy - Nileus - singing, followed by Tiresias.

NILEUS:(sings)   This clear blue sky,
               Delights the eye,
               And shows the mind unclouded.
               For we are free,
               To think and be,
               And soar in realms unbounded.

               For we take wing,
               Where no birds sing,
               And care not for the 'morrow.
               Delighting in,
               This realm within,
               We leap this world of sorrow.

               Oh this clear blue sky,
               Delights the eye,
               And fills our thoughts with wonder.
               For we can be,
               Forever free,
               To dwell within its splendour.

TIRESIAS: What song is this boy?

NILEUS: The words are yours, recited o'er the years,
               The tune came in my head as we have climbed.

TIRESIAS: Well done! Always pay your inspiration heed.
               Where are we now? What landscape are we in?

NILEUS: A rocky wasteland on a mountain path,
               That leads us high above the plains of Thebes.
               Behind us lies King Laius in his court,
               Roaring out his madness to the sky.
               Before us, lies the road to Pelops' fort,
               While far below, the battlefield - now still -
               Where their respective armies fought for naught.

TIRESIAS: Ha!

Halfway between two madmen stand the sane!
This air is pure, yet no birds soar or sing.
Why is this so?

NILEUS: The evening sky is pulling on its cloak;
Whose velvet red, called sunset, warms the west,
While over to the east its black fur hood,
Draws down the darker richness of the night.
No birds will soar or sing at this still time,
For spirits from the nether regions rise,
Seeking out some place to work their spells,
And plague the world with mischief and disease.
We too, must stop ere long, before the Dark,
Wraps us in its mantle for the night,
And gently snuffs the source of our day's light.

TIRESIAS: Be not afraid of this my little one.
My nightly vigil will ensure your peaceful sleep.
You are my eyes throughout these long bright days,
While I watch over you through night's long dark.
Be not afraid, the gods are with us now.

NILEUS: With you, no doubt.
You slipped into a trance some two miles back,
And stood transfixed for many a lengthy hour,
Crying out some words I did not know,
And ending every speech with screams of woe.

TIRESIAS: A trance you say? So that explains the time.
And yet you claim that I cried out in pain?

NILEUS: You did, indeed!

TIRESIAS: Then did I utter nothing you recall?

NILEUS: Nothing. Nothing but... 'Chrysippus and Oedipus'.
Those names you yelled aloud,
Shrieking out each syllable with pain.

TIRESIAS: Chrysippus and Oedipus you say? Mmn.
And that is all?

NILEUS: That's all. Or all that I recall.
You gabbled on so fast I oft was lost,
As one sound chased the other into space,
Like rolling rocks which tumble o'er this cliff,

69

And reach the ground before we see them fall.

TIRESIAS: Oedipus and Chrysippus? How stood they in this world?

NILEUS: They were unev'nly matched, or so it seemed,
              For Oedipus was loud and strong of voice,
              While Chrysippus, far gentler in his tones,
              And seemed the more submissive of the two.

TIRESIAS: And how did they relate?

NILEUS: At times it seemed a dialogue ensued,
              Proceeding in some ritual 'tween this pair.
              One tried to make the other share his view
              By bearing down upon him with great force,
              And crushing his resistance in one blow.

TIRESIAS: What happened then?

NILEUS: The gentle one but let this force flow by,
              And opened up his heart with depthless love,
              Waiting like a vessel to be filled.

TIRESIAS: And then?

NILEUS: The softer being made headway with this ploy.
              For soon the cruder aspect seemed to sway,
              And would have fall'n full-bodied in his arms,
              Had not some power of darkness then approached.

TIRESIAS: And you could tell all this just from my voice?

NILEUS: I had not thought to question it before.

TIRESIAS: Then do so now.
              Recall once more the phases of my trance.

NILEUS: (slowly) You stood transfixed, so I sat down to wait,
              Mindful lest you do yourself some harm.
              {Though well I know you never move one hair,
              Nor breathe one breath until the fit departs.}
              And then their voices crept into my brain...
              No. More than that. I saw them at this game...
              The court of Pelops... Some cool, lofty room...
              One man alone in agony cries out.
              Then you are there... Or rather... not as you,

70

But in some other shape which I knew not -
Some boy, who seemed to glow with golden light.
And then some darkness came upon that place,
And blotted out my vision of the scene.

TIRESIAS: I've taught you well, my faithful, guiding, friend,
You have become a seer, just like myself.

NILEUS: But how could this occur?

TIRESIAS: Tis eas'ly told.
The passing on of power from mind to mind.
For many years you've been my eyes and ears,
My contact with the colours of this world.
While I to you impart my inner realm,
Where images and dreams become more real,
Than any of the sights you daily see.
I live in formless landscapes full of forms,
That shift and change their aspects as they will,
Where emptiness becomes the only prop,
That underwrites the substance of their skill.
My meditation takes me to these realms,
And you partake, by virtue of your love.

NILEUS: You mean, that just being with you, I become,
What you, in your deep conscious, always are?

TIRESIAS: Perhaps.
And, as we grow together, I am you.

NILEUS: But who were all these people that I saw,
And can we help them ease their dreadful plight?

TIRESIAS: One cannot change, what does not wish to change.
We offered help, the choice - indeed - was theirs,
But they refused;
Preferring in their weakness, what they knew,
Than venturing to taste the vast unknown.
Their future's set. Their actions have been made.
There's nothing we can do to help them now.

NILEUS: Then are they doomed?

TIRESIAS: Be calm awhile. I'll answer by and by.
One never dies completely to the Good.
Let's first of all find shelter from the night.

Tis time that we were from this place, long gone.
Lead on and sing again your pretty song.

(Exit Nileus singing followed by Tiresias.)

END OF ACT 1 SCENE 6

ACT 1 SCENE 7

A dark but moonlit night. A rocky valley. The time approaching midnight. Several soldiers stand round, on guard. enter Laius and Lysias.

LAIUS: (*shouts*) Captain?

PROTEUS: Here, my liege.

LAIUS: Is all prepared?

PROTEUS: The letter of your law has been obeyed.
             The men are all set round, as you detailed,
             To guard your royal presence with their lives.
             They form concentric circles from this spot,
             Arcing out from one rich central core,
             Like rings, that are discovered in a trunk,
             And show the many ages of a tree.
             Our youngest troops, are furthest from the heart,
             - Their recklessness will keep the foe at bay -
             While those around this spot, are seasoned men,
             Who prove their worth by living through the fray.

LAIUS: Good.
             Then if this be a trap, we are prepared,
             And will reverse its spring upon our foes.

PROTEUS: There is no way their army can approach
             Without them first encountering our scouts.
             And even then, on this unkind terrain,
             They'd only send their men in ones or twos,
             Not drown us in the deluge of their hordes.

LAIUS: Good! Then thus far are we safe.
             She is a cunning woman of a witch,
             To choose this spot to meet on such a night;
             A valley that has openings on all sides,
             Where she may slip and slither like an eel,
             That cannot be confined to one still spot.
             I curse the scheming blackness of her mind.

PROTEUS: At least this moon will show us where she comes.

LAIUS:	I think this moon's too full for such a tryst. Dark deeds deserve dark settings to enshroud, The evil which their blackness will arouse. How goes the hour?
PROTEUS:	Tis almost twelve my lord.
LAIUS:	What think you Proteus, will she come on time?
PROTEUS:	T'would be most unbecoming of her sex, To grace us with the honour of her being, Before at least the quarter hour had struck.
LAIUS:	Her sex is graceless, if the gossip's true. *(They laugh.)*
PROTEUS:	She shows great courage, coming here tonight, Into the very heart of our domain.
LAIUS:	A witch like her, has little need to fear, Being that herself, which fills us full of fear. How will she know to find us when she comes?
PROTEUS:	Cretheus and Pelias patrol, The furthest reaches of this ring of men, And will, when she has made her presence known, Conducted her to this spot with utmost speed.
LAIUS:	What of the men, what reason do they have, That keeps them on their guard through this long night?
PROTEUS:	They willingly manoeuvre in the dark, Knowing you are present on the field, And think no more than that we do rehearse, Some tactic we may use against our foe.
LAIUS:	Tis well. No word of this affair must reach their ranks. Lysias, what fancy draws your eye?
LYSIAS:	Look my lord. See how the moon goes falling through those clouds, As if it would depart these heavenly shores, And travel free across unbounded space, To rid itself forever of our woes.

74

LAIUS:	I loathe these nights, when shapes and shades assume,
	All manner of importance to the brain.
	I n'er can feel at ease in this dark state,
	But see before me, spectres from my past,
	Which rise with such abundance from this earth,
	They overwhelm the reason of my being.
LYSIAS:	Be not afeared. They will not do you harm.
	They are but rich imaginings at work.
	These spectres that you see are merely rocks,
	That alter as the radiance of the moon
	Casts its milky whiteness o'er the earth.
LAIUS:	You foolish youth!
	I know when shadows form unearthly shapes,
	And when imagination flies too far.
	Do not proceed to lecture me on this.
LYSIAS:	Forgive me, sire, I only meant to soothe,
	Not lecture you on things you know full well.
	I had the best intentions in my heart,
	For oft your mind gets locked into this state,
	And causes you such anguish and such pain,
	That I can not abide to see you so.
LAIUS:	Sweet foolish boy,
	You worry over-greatly for my health,
	And I have done you wrong to chide you thus.
	Pay no heed to my mood,
	This waiting aggravates my heated brain,
	And drives me into curtness with my tongue.
	I'm nervous of the night,
	And wish the sun would bathe us in its light.
	But hush! I hear a noise.
PROTEUS:	Tis Cretheus, I recognise his gait.
	(Enter Cretheus.)
	Cretheus!
CRETHEUS:	Proteus. My liege.
LAIUS:	What word on this affair?
CRETHEUS:	I've checked the outer limit of our guard,

	And all is still.
	But yet there are some gaps where one or two,
	May slip between the net of our defence.
PROTEUS:	We've set them thus, that she may find a route,
	And leave behind whatever guard she brings,
	Before advancing too far through our ranks.
LAIUS:	So be it. Let her come alone.
	Why may we not indeed revise our plans,
	And be much less defensive than we are,
	Attacking them when they would least expect?
PROTEUS:	My lord, we are not armoured for attack!
LAIUS:	No. No. I'm musing to myself.
	I gave my word. We'll let her come in peace,
	Although we may regret it 'fore too long.
	I more incline to learn of her dark plot,
	Than give my eager sanction to her death.
	What noise is that?
PROTEUS:	Tis but an owl my lord.
	Screeching through the silence of the night.
	They hunt this hour, when blackness is complete,
	Drawing in the darkness to their eyes,
	And filtering what little light remains,
	To frame their helpless victim in their sight.

(The stage darkens noticeably)

LAIUS:	The moon goes in. I like this not.
PROTEUS:	Hush, some figures come our way.

(Enter Pelias and Hippodamia disguised in a heavy cloak and hood.)

PELIAS:	*(Approaching)* This way my liege, our majesty awaits.
LAIUS:	Hippodamia.
HIPPODAMIA:	King Laius.
LAIUS:	We have not met before, but I can see,
	Nobility of birth in your slim grace,

76

And recognise the line of royal descent,
That harks back to your father's noble clan.
Those inky lines, which introduced us first,
Hinted at fine features in your face,
But hid the nat'ral beauty of your looks.

HIPPODAMIA: Good sir!
Let's make no useless show of feeble praise,
Or stand upon the ceremonies due.
Our business militates against such acts.
My hair is black. My face is pale and plain.
My father was the king of distant lands.
Therefore, make an end of further lies.

LAIUS: I stand chastised.

HIPPODAMIA: Then let us to the business of this night.

LAIUS: Indeed,
We'll step aside in private for a while.
Proteus. Watch well.
This dark contains far more than meets the eye.

PROTEUS: *(To Laius)* Too true!
That lady has a viper in her tongue!

LAIUS: *(To Proteus)* I think the viper's tongue is not so sharp.
(aloud) Watch well!

(Hippodamia and Laius stand apart.)

Your letter hinted ways we might collude,
To benefit each other through some pact,
And mentioned mutual means, we might employ
To bring about an end to this long war,
Which drains both lives, and riches, from our lands.

HIPPODAMIA: That was, indeed, the content of my note.
I know, as well as you, this war has raged,
Too long for either side to make it theirs.
There is, in both our countries, discontent,
And each new day, new rebel leaders rise,
Who claim that kings are tyrants and abuse,
The rights of common people with their power.
These rebels soon incite vast rowdy mobs,
To launch ill-timed assaults upon our court,

And hope to overthrow us with such coups.
We, in our Kingdom, spend more time on them,
Than fighting with our more acknowledged foes.
I know that you do likewise in your state.

LAIUS: Tis true. We have, at times, to quell a mob.

HIPPODAMIA: Such rowdy mobs can make or break a reign.
My plan is but to guarantee our right -
A right all royal blood must surely have -
To rule our mutual kingdoms as we choose,
Not live in fear of death at ev'ry turn.

LAIUS: Go on,
Your words thus far, have all made perfect sense.

HIPPODAMIA: I can, if you accede to my full plan,
Make Pelops see the sense of such a course,
And set in motion, from this very night,
The overtures to bring about this peace.
For I have gathered round me all those men -
Potential rebels for the people's cause -
Who wish to bring about this state of change,
And they are waiting, restless for my word,
To realise in peace what they desire,
But thought could only come through blood and death.

LAIUS: You seem a better statesman than the king.

HIPPODAMIA: He dreams o'er much to rule his kingdom well.
What think you of this plan?

LAIUS: Simplicity itself.
You set in motion reasons for a peace,
Dispatching eager envoys to our court.
We hear their pleas, and welcome them as friends,
Meeting to agree our mutual terms.
Then, when the people hear that peace is made
They'll no more seek to rise against our power.
And thus,
Combined in peace, our countries thrive and grow,
And blossom in this more conducive life.
But what - apart from this,
Which in itself is almost fruit enough -
Will I have gained, and what do you desire?

HIPPODAMIA: I know this war began o'er some small state,
Which both sides claim is theirs, by right, to take.
That land, I will ensure is passed to you,
When deeds and treaties to this peace are drawn.
I'll also see that gold from my estate,
Supplements your income for a year.
For my part here, I have but simple needs.
I am the loving mother of two sons
And want for them the best that life can bring.
Their father has departed from this life,
And Pelops, though he plays the father's part,
Is more concerned to nurture his true son.
This boy, who is a demon in disguise,
Forever shows my sons in such poor light,
That Pelops in his fury oft has thought
To bar them from the legacy they're due.
To seal our friendship in this pact of peace,
Your part will be to rid me of this boy.

LAIUS: Kill Pelops' son!
Why, if he met his death upon my sword,
That would be cause enough to start once more,
This bloody war we're seeking here to end.

HIPPODAMIA: Have patience yet.
I shall contrive the boy will visit you,
To seal this peace and show we mean good faith.
While in your court he'll meet with some foul death -
The details, in good time, you may arrange ...

LAIUS: WHAT??...

HIPPODAMIA: Be still awhile and hear me to the end.
I shall be present with him in your court,
Again, as proof this peace is meant to last,
When he will meet his most untimely death.

LAIUS: Then you will vouch he died not at my hands.

HIPPODAMIA: Indeed I shall.
His death will seem an 'accident', to those,
Who hear, from my own tongue, just how he died.
(This tale we will rehearse at greater length,
When time is more propitious than 'tis now.)
And you will back this story to the hilt,
Thus proving that no malice was abroad.

LAIUS: And Pelops?

HIPPODAMIA: He will, at first, be overcome with grief,
                But I can pacify his broken heart,
                And clarify the story, should he doubt,
                That any other circumstance prevailed.

LAIUS: This seems a bloody way to reach a peace.

HIPPODAMIA: Two lives for thousands? Surely this is cheap?

LAIUS: Two? What two? We have discussed but one.

HIPPODAMIA: The other is a simple act of war.
                We had a soldier, Oedipus by name...

LAIUS: I know it.
                Our troops speak very highly of this youth.

HIPPODAMIA: He was, by all accounts a valiant youth,
                Until his manly pride undid his sense.

LAIUS: What do you mean?

HIPPODAMIA: Some days ago, before this last affray,
                T'was rumoured he'd deserted from our ranks,
                And shown a coward's yellowness at heart.
                Then he was heard no more, till late last night,
                When I was rudely woken by his voice.
                He burst into the chamber, where I slept,
                And brandishing his sword to prove his words,
                Declared he was the bravest man alive,
                I tried to reason with him for a while,
                But he was drunk, and threw me from my bed,
                Attempting to assault me there and then.
                I screamed aloud! My handmaid came at once,
                Preserving me from further vile assaults,
                And thus disturbed, he blundered from the room,
                Screaming like a man possessed with fiends,
                And vanished from the precinct of our court.
                Today I've learned, he is on board a ship,
                Bound for Delphi's shrine to seek some peace,
                And hide among the pilgrims gathered there.
                I beg you, send some men to cut him down,
                That I may have revenge upon this cur.

LAIUS:	By why not have your own troops take his life? Such cowardice deserves an instant death. King Pelops' sword, should soon dispatch with haste, A man who tried to rape his loyal wife.
HIPPODAMIA:	Oh! Herein lies my pain. And shows the foolish weakness of my sex. I cannot tell my spouse this fault occurred, Or he would have me banished from his court.
LAIUS:	Banished?
HIPPODAMIA:	Oh. A woman's role is seldom understood. Pelops would disown me if he knew, That some rough, common, soldier touched my flesh, And made a hot assault upon my self. He has a most unnatural belief, 'bout cleanliness and functions of the flesh, Claiming that all death, is but at root, Some unclean skin which passes on its rot. He will not touch my children, nor his son, Until they are anointed at a shrine.
LAIUS:	This seems unnatural prejudice indeed!
HIPPODAMIA:	It is. In one so kind and gentle, such belief, Seems monstrous, and far worse than any crime, Than that foul fiend could hope to have achieved. But then, The sum of Pelops' goodness, far outweighs, The aberrant behaviour of this lapse. We tolerate the strangest faults for love.
LAIUS:	Tis true. We do indeed.
HIPPODAMIA:	But tell me that you will revenge my pain. If I were not a mother, I would go, And cut my own sweet vengeance from his flesh.
LAIUS:	Be calm. I'll send some men to carry out this deed.
HIPPODAMIA:	Induce them into secrecy I pray, Lest Pelops ever hears what did befall.

	Make it seem they killed him as their foe,
	Recognised from battles on this plain.
LAIUS:	Control your grief. I'll have them frame it so.
	Distress yourself no more. You'll have revenge.
HIPPODAMIA:	Your kindness lifts my heart from so much pain.
	But come, I must away.
	I should be safely back before the dawn
	Or all our plans will shrivel into naught.
	You do agree to all we have discussed?
LAIUS:	I do.
HIPPODAMIA:	Good. Then I shall go.
	Tomorrow will begin a new regime,
	Of peace and mutual trust between our states.
LAIUS:	Pelias!
	Escort the queen back safely to her lines,
	Ensuring that the soldiers see her not.
	Protect her well, from any sign of threat,
	Your life will be the price, should she be harmed.
PELIAS:	I'll gladly die, protecting such a ward.
	I brought her here in safety through our ranks,
	And pride myself I can return her thus.
	Come Madame.
	Take my hand. The ground is somewhat rough.
HIPPODAMIA:	*(She looks at Laius)*
	I'll steer my own course if you please.
	Adieu, good King,
	And may we meet again in better times.
LAIUS:	Adieu good lady.
	May the gods go with you. Adieu!
CRETHEUS:	*(To Proteus)* He seems quite overawed by all her charm.
PROTEUS:	*(To Cretheus)* She has bewitched him with her evil tongue.
LYSIAS:	Good sir, you look distraught.
LAIUS:	No Lysias, just musing on the mystery of Life.
	What strange affairs the lives of others are,

We little know the suffering each endures.
The rumours paint that woman as a witch,
But I have seen a kind and loving wife;
A mother; and a frightened virgin girl;
All living in that mask of royal calm.
We do each other wrong to judge in haste,
The outward face presented to the world.
We should not rush to call our foe, a fiend,
Because we only see him as our foe.
But come, enough of this. Let's to our beds.
These sleepless nights will dog us through our days.
Farewell, good Captains. Give the men my cheer,
And not a word of this to any ear.

PROTEUS: & CRETHEUS: *(together)* No, my liege.

LAIUS: Farewell.

(Exit Laius and Lysias)

CRETHEUS: Now there's a load of thanks!
Four hundred men arrayed around this hill,
To guard his royal hide from wild attack.
And off he goes, without a nod or wink,
To indicate what all this was about.

PROTEUS: We do not serve to know our master's mind.
Come. Let's get these men dismissed.
The dawn will soon be rising in the east,
And I for one, am eager for my bed,
Where pleasant dreams can purge this from my head.

(Exit all.)

END OF ACT 1 SCENE 7

END OF ACT ONE

ACT 2 SCENE 1

Night. A desolate heath. enter Livia bearing a lamp, carrying a spade, and followed by Thyestes dragging a bundle along the ground.

THYESTES: Livia! Livia! Don't go so far ahead.

                You know I fear the dark.

LIVIA: Then keep in step you weak-willed, whining, brat.
Your help has been more trouble than it's worth.
And hold that bag up high,
You drag it on the ground like some old sack;
Show some respect at least.

THYESTES: Oh let's go back.
My legs are weary, and I want my bed.
I'm tired of playing this silly game with you.

LIVIA: Beshrew your lips! You think I like this job:
Tramping through this wilderness at night?
We do it for your mother, not for me.
So hold your carping tongue and take more care,
And keep that bag from bumping on the ground!

THYESTES: You've lied! You rotten, scheming, bitch!
You said this whole adventure was for you,
And if I came, I'd get a good reward.
Why did you lead me on with such a lie,
If you did not intend to see it through?

LIVIA: Would you have done it if I'd told the truth,
Or begged your kind assistance in this deed?
No. Not you, you ball of mewlish pap!
You would have feigned some sickness of the heart,
And languished like a Lover on his bed
Pretending that some ague seared your flesh.
Now take that spade and dig a good-sized hole.
We'll lose this loathsome load within the earth,
And then begone. Here. *(she hands him the spade.)*
I'll hold the light and watch lest we're disturbed.

THYESTES: Oh no you don't, you haughty, lying, wench.
'Tis all your fault that we have ended here,

	Flailing in this stench infested den.
	I'll hold the light, and you can dig the hole.
	Your arms are more accustomed to this work,
	And digging suits your station more than mine.

LIVIA: You turgid, spineless, brat!
You have not half your mother's strength.
Give me that spade! I'll show you how to dig,
And bury you along with all this strife! (*she digs.*)

THYESTES: Dig well, it suits your low estate.
I don't know why I bother with your kind,
You're nothing but a peasant through and through.
One day I'll have the choice of all this land,
And rid myself of sluttish, serving, whores.

LIVIA: The ground is soft we'll soon be out of here.
Don't dally with that bag and hold the lantern still.
You throw more shadows than a fading flame.

THYESTES: What's in this bag that makes you so irate,
And drags us from the court at dead of night?
Some hidden treasure from my mother's room?
Some golden trinkets from my father's tomb?

LIVIA: Just leave it there. And shine that light o'er here,
I'm digging in the dark.

THYESTES: What's in this bag? You'd better tell me now,
Or I will leave you stranded on your own.

LIVIA: Oh scrawny, wretched, whelp!
Put down that bag before I put you down.

THYESTES: Ha! I'll put you up, before you put me down.

(he grabs her)

LIVIA: Get off! We're here to do a job.

THYESTES: I'm game. This is the kind of job I like to do.

(she pushes him away)

LIVIA: Grow up!
Do you know nothing but your own desires?

THYESTES: Nothing! (*he advances.*)

LIVIA: Off! (*she pushes him away he trips over the bag.*)

THYESTES: Bitch!
              I'll spill the hidden secrets of this sack.

              (*he tips the contents of the bag out*)

              Eugh! What's this? A bag of blood and gore!
              What sick unfunny joke of yours, is this?
              Have we tramped way out here to bury that?

              (*she grabs the bag returns the contents and closes it.*)

LIVIA: Put up this sight, 'tis not for eyes like yours.

THYESTES: What is that thing, that wallows in this sack?

LIVIA: Do you know nothing of the facts of life,
              Or are you blind to all but your own cares?

THYESTES: I know enough to know what fun they are.
              Come here, (*he grabs her waist*)
              I'll show you what I know.
              We could make pretty babies in this grass,
              And bump away our time until the dawn.

LIVIA: Get off! One baby is enough for one dark night!

THYESTES: A baby? What do you mean?
              Is that some bloody baby in this bag?

              (*He looks in the bag again.*)

LIVIA: Just shut the neck and throw it in the hole.

THYESTES: No! Tell me what it is?

LIVIA: You have no need to know.

THYESTES: I need to know, and you will tell me now!

              (*he twists her arm*)

86

LIVIA: Ahh! Let go. You're twisting on my arm.

THYESTES: Then tell me what it is?

LIVIA: A baby, like I said.

THYESTES: A baby? A bloody, baby child?
              You common slut!
              Have you been whoring while my back was turned,
              And spawned this ugly brat to someone else?
              Tell me!

LIVIA: Let go my arm, you're twisting it right sore.

THYESTES: Then tell me what I ask!

LIVIA: Thyestes, let go! Ahh!

THYESTES: Then tell me what it is?

LIVIA: A still born baby from your mother's womb,
              Made through sport 'tween Lucien and her.
              (she breaks free.) Ahh!
              There! Now you know. You cruel, ungrateful, beast.

THYESTES: No! This is not true! You lie to save yourself.
              My mother is not like some common slut,
              Who gives her body to the nearest man
              To foul her sheets and fill her womb with pain...

LIVIA: Then why has she been locked up in her room,
              Confined to bed,
              And seeing not a soul these past few weeks?

THYESTES: She had a fever. All the court knew that.

LIVIA: Aye. A fever of passion.

THYESTES: No! This is not true.
              I cannot see my mother in this role,
              A common, cheating whore, and yet a Queen?

LIVIA: Bear up. Are Queens not human too?

THYESTES: But what about her screams at dead of night?

LIVIA: Screams of guilt that haunt her sleepless nights,
For bloody deeds committed long ago.
Since she became full-blown with this dead child,
Her mind has been a sea of sad remorse.
She spends her days in converse with the dead
Talking to her father and your sire,
As if they both still walked upon this earth.
She rages 'gainst all happiness and joy,
And Chrysippus gets blamed for every fault.

THYESTES: No!
This cannot be her senses are quite sound.

LIVIA: Your mother is so clouded in her thought,
She knows not right from wrong.
She flits between her self-constructed realms,
Playing so many parts in one short hour,
She knows not what is real and what is not.

THYESTES: You lie!
You spread these tales to ease your sense of guilt.
This child is yours. You cheating, rotten, whore!

LIVIA: *(she slaps him.)* Enough!
The truth is told. I warned you not to look.
So shut your gawking mouth and ask no more.
And never breathe the slightest breath of this,
Or we will all lie buried on this heath.
Now help me get this creature in the ground,
Then we'll be off.

THYESTES: No. I will not be contaminated thus.
You fill it in. I will not touch it more.
You cannot bury truth like bloody babes.
One day his tongue will find its own revenge.

(she fills in the hole.)

LIVIA: You weak and spineless creature that you are,
Usurper of the name and state of Man.
Come. Let's go in.
I'm sick of night, of birth, and death, and you.

(they exit in silence.)

END OF ACT 2 SCENE 1

ACT 2 SCENE 2

Lais' palace wall, night. occasional sounds of festive drum and trumpet off. - enter Proteus

PROTEUS: Cretheus?

CRETHEUS: Ah Proteus 'tis you. And not before you're due.

PROTEUS: How goes your watch?

CRETHEUS: Long and slow.
As if this night had crushed the wings of Time,
And never would release me from this spot.

PROTEUS: Be not so sour. You knew that I would come.
I merely stopped to quaff a glass or two,
With some young wench encountered in the street,
Ecstatic in her praise of this new peace.

CRETHEUS: New Peace! 'Tis almost three months old!

PROTEUS: *(He takes a deep breath.)* Ahh!
This gentle air is warm and full of light,
And should make pleasant watching till the dawn.

CRETHEUS: Aye. Warm and light like wine,
That makes our brain insensible to sense.
This heavy air hangs coldly round my head,
Stunk sickly with the scent of perfumed fruit
From all the festal frolics of the court.
Three months of peace have made our people mad,
Rejoicing every night that war is o'er,
As if there's no tomorrow yet to come.
These trumpets and the beating of yon drum
Have proved a source of torment to my skull,
Banging out their rhythms all night long.
I'd rather hear the sound of steel on steel
Than have this joyful madness break my ears.

PROTEUS: Oh say not so.
There was a time when you cried out for peace,
And longed to be rejoicing till the dawn.
Oft times we wished that we were back in court
Not fretful of our lives upon that field.

90

| | Cheer up. Be happy with your lot. |
| | Don't waste this chance of freedom, mourning war. |

CRETHEUS: We're soldiers man! Not nursemaids to the sick!
Our country's gone insane with all this peace,
And squanders all our hard-won gains in feasts,
That make our courtiers fat, and coffers lean.
Did we do ten years battle just for this?

PROTEUS: Cretheus!
What makes your tongue lash out with so much ire?
Our people are triumphant. All is well.
And we are given prosperity and health.
Yet you'd prefer to wallow in this gloom,
Than face the happy changes that occur.

CRETHEUS: This is not gloom, but sober sense that sees,
The evil that will plague us 'fore too long.
Think you on this, my friend.
That Chrysippus - our former foe's sole son -
So bends the ear of Laius to his whims,
That he dictates the statutes that are drawn.
He fills this court with all his wild ideas,
'Bout wisdom and the perfect state of man.
Till no one dares to question what it means
Nor how his thought ensnares us in some plot,
Which will at last prove fatal to us all!

PROTEUS: Oh Cretheus,
Your mind is too embittered by this war.
How you see any evil in his thought
I cannot comprehend!
Be not so narrow in your point of view.
The boy is young, and full of Life's delights.
His youthful vision holds no trace of harm,
But fills our court with joy and future hopes.
Already by his words our lot's improved
And many of our troops have left their ranks
To benefit themselves in other trades.
Where is the wrong in kindness and concern?

CRETHEUS: See you not the treachery in this?
Our greatest foe,
Now harboured in the bosom of our court,
And granted constant access to our King,
Dismantles all our army piece by piece,

Till one day soon his father will appear,
And strike us dead, as we lie in our sleep.

PROTEUS: Oh Cretheus,
              Your morbid nature feeds on false beliefs.
              This boy is like some angel in disguise,
              Sent here to heal our wounds and make us strong.
              There is no trace of malice in his thought.
              He's like some ancient god when'er he speaks
              A god our people lost too long ago.
              Look at all the good his words have done.
              Our country is ablaze with joy and hope,
              The King, so optimistic in his reign,
              That we should be rejoicing with the mob,
              To be alive at this rich point in time.
              If we fulfil one fraction of this hope,
              We will transform, not only our own Thebes,
              But all the isles and countryside of Greece:
              Create the greatest empire known to man;
              Abolish hatred; rid ourselves of greed;
              And spend our earthly years, like heavenly gods!
              Does not this hopeful vision warm your heart?

CRETHEUS: I see, you too, are poisoned by his tongue,
              Made dupe to all the nonsense of his scheme.
              This boy will prove the downfall of our state,
              Bring discontent, and internecine strife.
              He undermines the nature of our life,
              Turns topsy-turvy all our natural laws,
              And ranks both kings and servants all as one.
              If he should gain more power than he has,
              What will our roles as Captains then become?

PROTEUS: What fear you here? He does not seek our rank.
              Or any of the attributes of power!
              You fail to comprehend his simple thought,
              Preferring selfish falsehood to the truth!
              He claims all men are equal in their hearts,
              Regardless of their power, place, or pomp;
              And therefore mighty Kings, as well as serfs,
              Must strive to make this world a better place,
              Where lies the threat in that?

CRETHEUS: I say he is a curse, sent here to bring us down,
              And I'll be ready, when he makes his move,
              To end the sickly sweetness of his smile.

PROTEUS: Then you will kill the saviour of our state.

CRETHEUS: Aye, that I will, and mercilessly.

PROTEUS: Cretheus!
              Are you so scared of change that you'll destroy,
              The very thing we've fought for all these years?
              Have we not spent our lives upon that field,
              Fighting for our Freedom; Peace and Truth?
              And now, when we've a chance to make them live,
              You'd snuff them out before they start to breathe.

CRETHEUS: I only kill when I perceive some threat.
              You are too drunk, like all our reeling state,
              To see this deadly viper at our breast.
              This boy will undermine our country's laws!
              Be dumb! Be deaf! Be blind to all his faults,
              And let him stamp upon you as he will.
              I'll not desert you when his colours show,
              Though you desert me now, while yet he sleeps.

PROTEUS: This o'er-long watch has filled you full of ire.
              We cannot solve this quarrel here and now.
              Go in dear friend, and rest your weary head,
              I would not have you agitated more.

CRETHEUS: I'll gladly go.
              These sleepless nights, and this loud, tuneless drum,
              Combine to fill my head with throbbing pain.
              Give careful thought to all that I have said,
              We'll argue on this matter, come the dawn.
              Farewell.
              And may your watch prove shorter than did mine.

PROTEUS: Farewell!

              (Cretheus exits.)

              Poor fool.
              He tries in vain to stem what's Good and True,
              Because he does not wish to change his life.
              Let's hope there are not many share his view,
              Or we'll be plunged once more in endless strife.

              (He exits.)

93

END OF ACT 2 SCENE 2

ACT 2 SCENE 3

A chamber in the court of Thebes. Jocasta is wearing the shawl from ACT 1 SCENE 3.

JOCASTA: Sweet Lysias,
I'm grateful for your counsel and concern,
Your comfort o'er these months has proved a boon,
But I'm a woman, mother of a child,
Earth Goddess to the dictates of my womb.
How can you comprehend my depth of woe?
You have no urges like we women have;
To bear, to nurture, suckle into life,
How can you hope to soothe these gnawing needs,
Which tear the very fabric of my flesh?
For I still crave the pleasures of a man:
The strength; the warmth; the comfort of his love.
I long to find a husband I can mould,
And turn upon this world to rule for me,
Not play the stooge to some ungrateful King!
You're sweet and kind, gentle and refined,
But cannot fill the dictates of this role,
And I must therefore languish in this hell,
Sexless, loveless, lustful and forlorn.

LYSIAS: Oh madam do not make yourself so ill.
Your chastity is famed throughout our land,
And proves a moral standard for us all.

JOCASTA: My chastity's a curse that I endure,
Because I dare not break my marriage vows!
Oh how I long to rid me of this pain,
To taste once more the joy that men can bring,
Not be forever chained to barren laws.
Can you not share the sourness of my fate,
And sympathize more clearly with my loss,
Now Laius dotes so madly on that boy,
And casts you out so rudely from his bed?

LYSIAS: I know full well Rejection's icy smart,
And sympathize completely with your plight,
And wish that I could soothe your aching heart.

JOCASTA: Then join with me and wreak some wild revenge.

95

Let's tear this latest lover from his arms,
Like he once tore the babe that I adored.

LYSIAS: No!
             Your words are lunar, tainted with despair;
             And full of moony madness and deceit!
             I bear the King no malice, nor would harm,
             This boy who has replaced me in his love,
             For he is but a simple, honest child.

JOCASTA: You are not jealous that he steals your place,
             And wriggles in those sheets that once were yours?

LYSIAS: No!
             He is a good companion for the King,
             And he and I have grown to be good friends,
             While Laius is more tender with me now
             Than ever in the heyday of our Love.

JOCASTA: Then you have never felt True Love's full power!
             When Laius held me tightly on that night,
             I knew at once that he and I were one,
             Both born to be united through our love.
             That feeling of completeness we attained,
             Made sense of all my yearnings o'er the years,
             And filled me with a wholeness so sublime,
             That I was bathed in ecstasies divine.
             But Laius, 'fore that rosy dawn crept in,
             Resumed his former state and cast me out;
             Denied me this rich aspect of myself,
             And made my life a barren, joyless, hell.
             Oh, had I but the courage of my thought,
             I should have plunged my knife into his heart,
             Relieving my resentment there and then.
             For now I lack a purpose in this life,
             And crave, with all my heart, to be fulfilled,
             By someone who denies that I exist.
             Can you see now, the horror I endure?

LYSIAS: (He hugs her to him)
             Oh gentle Queen, do not re-live this past.
             I wish that I could ease you of this pain,
             And soothe your lonely days with loving balm.

JOCASTA: (She breaks free)
             You cannot! For you know not what love is!

96

LYSIAS: You claim I do not know the power of love,
            But I have felt a love as strong as yours;
            Have tasted pleasure in a thousand ways,
            And been an equal partner in delight.
            I loved the King, and know that he loved me,
            And when this boy first stole his heart away
            My thoughts, like yours, turned murderous and sour,
            And fed themselves on ravage and revenge.
            But I did not allow these seeds of hate,
            To fester in my bosom and grow old,
            Stinking like the stench of rotting flesh.
            I plucked them out, and threw them to the air,
            Made riddance all this hindrance to my heart.
            For Love, like all our frailties, fades and dies,
            And we must lose those bonds that we have made
            Which bind us, through dependence, to our loves.
            For though our hearts may break when first we part,
            We gain our independence from this blight.
            Are free to live our lives and love again.
            Tis folly to be ruled by someone else,
            And base one's whole existence on their love.
            Shake off these chains that bind you to this mood,
            Become again the woman that you are,
            Not merely some dull shadow of the king.

JOCASTA: Oh would that I could make myself so free.
            Your words are easy, for your heart is young,
            And able to find other hearts to love.
            But I am trapped, enslavéd to this man,
            And suffer for the crime of being true!
            For he is mine, and I still want his love,
            Desire the satisfaction love can bring,
            And loathe this barren desert I endure.
            I cannot live forever chaste and pure!

LYSIAS: Oh madam do not rack your feelings so,
            You have no right to treat yourself this way.

JOCASTA: Right! Right!
            I am his wife! Does this not give me right?

LYSIAS: Mere right of law!
            You are a woman, lovely to behold.
            A Queen. A cherished presence in our land.
            Do not deny the virtue you contain,

Or make your lofty station seem so low.
You are yourself, and should rejoice in that,
Not crave to be a part in someone else.
Shake off these foolish notions that you hold,
And think no more of him.
He neither can, nor will, return your love,
For he has turned his back on women's charms,
And seeks in youths, his pleasure and his love.

JOCASTA: A plague on all his house, and his foul love!
             Did I not feel entrapped by ties of blood,
             I'd run amok and kill all those he loves,
             That Chrysippus, those wanton boys, and you!
             But I endure, through weakness and dismay,
             And fill this humble role of faithful wife.
             So do not give me words of sound advice.
             I know what I must do.
             Hold high my pretty head to all the world,
             And wear this smiling mask that marks me wife;
             While in my breast the fragments of my heart,
             Cut deeper wounds with each new passing day.

             (She breaks down and cries.)

             Oh take me in, I am not fit to be.
             This latest youth, this Chrysippus, this prince,
             Has filled my place with such a sweet success
             That I can never hope to oust him now.

LYSIAS: Come, come. I'll take you to your room.
             And bring some balmy nectar for your hurt.
             This month has always caused you much distress.

JOCASTA: This month of pain. This month of endless pain.
             So many years have cradled this short month,
             This joyous month, this birth-month to a son.
             Oh golden son, sweet image of my womb,
             Oh how I would have filled you with my love,
             Had Laius not so cruelly had you killed.

LYSIAS: Be calm. Be calm.
             Your tears will not revitalize him now.

JOCASTA: No!
             My tears will not revitalize him now,
             But they can shed the guilt and pain I feel,

And scatter it like ashes o'er the ground,
And in this futile way relieve my heart.
But let's go in,
What use is there in howling out our cares,
When every ear is deaf to all our plight?
I shall not speak again of my distress,
But steel my heart to loneliness and pain.
Come, lead me in,
Your balm may chase this sadness from my brain.

(Exit Jocasta and Lysias.)

END OF ACT 2 SCENE 3

ACT 2 SCENE 4

*The rugged snowy mountain range containing mount Cithaeron.
enter Nileus leading Tiresias by the arm, Tiresias has a staff.
They proceed slowly and calmly along the snow-covered path.
then:*

OEDIPUS: *(Off)* Halt! Halt!

             (they stop and turn)

TIRESIAS: What man is that?

NILEUS: A stranger.
             With his sword unsheathed and anger in his eyes.

             *(Suddenly Oedipus appears brandishing a sword, he is out of
             breath and shouts.)*

OEDIPUS: Halt! Hold! Not one step more,
             Or Hades shall be host to your next tread.

NILEUS: *(Grabbing Tiresias' arm)* 'Tis he! 'Tis Oedipus!
             The figure from my dream.
             Is this another phantom that I see?

TIRESIAS: *(to Nileus)* No child, no. He's real enough,
             As real as Life's brief dream would have us be.
             I'll deal with him. He will not do us harm.
             (aloud) Who roars and shouts so loudly on this hill
             And threats his fellow travellers with doom?
             Declare yourself; your purpose, and your name!

OEDIPUS: Be still! Advance no more.
             My name need not concern you at this time.
             Just tell me, are you friend, or are you foe?

TIRESIAS: We are no foe, nor yet are we your friend.
             We're merely humble pilgrims, heading home,
             With news from Delphi's shrine to warm our kin.

OEDIPUS: That lying whore who curses all mankind,
             And taints my family ties with her vile breath!
             Keep still!

100

My sword is at the ready, mark my words.
Pilgrims you say?
Your tongue belies the action of your feet!
Three days I've run behind you on this trail,
Three days I've traced your tracks upon this snow
And never closed the gap between ourselves.
How can a lame old man and fretful boy
Walk at such a speed on this terrain
If you have not been trained as men of war?

TIRESIAS: Men of war?
Your mind is greatly fevered, my dear friend,
If two such, unarmed pilgrims, prove a threat,
To one who boasts so proudly of his sword.
The whiteness of this snow,
Has blinded you to simple facts of life.
Our hearts are light, and full of joyful thoughts,
That speed our feet to reach our journey's end,
While yours sound leaden-heavy with your woe,
And cannot match the lightness of our pace.

OEDIPUS: Tis true,
The curse of Delphi's robbed me of all hope,
And taught my feet the gait of Sorrow's weight.
And yet, you are no simple pilgrims as you claim.
This is no route to follow to your home.
What brings you here?

TIRESIAS: I could, with equal logic, ask of you
The answer to the question you pose me.
And yet,
This wind forbids me halting here too long,
Engaging in the Sophists' splitting art.
I am a hermit, and this boy my guide,
And Cithaeron is where we've made our home.
These tracks are daily comfort to our feet,
And hold no sense of mystery to us.
But what of you?
A man at war with all the world it seems.
Why not unload the torment from your breast,
Our ears will hear you through before we judge,
And may provide some peace for your wild storm?

OEDIPUS: Your voice is gentle, yet I trust it not,
This could be but a trap that's nearly sprung.

TIRESIAS:	*(turning away)* Come boy. This beast has left all human traits behind, And cannot tell what's true or what is false. *(Oedipus lunges at Tiresias and holds the tip of his sword to Tiresias' throat.)*
OEDIPUS:	Halt! no more! Your life if you speak more.
TIRESIAS:	Begone villain! You cannot take my life! I'll choose the time and place of my demise.
OEDIPUS:	You speak like one who little values life. Only a fool, or hermit, would ignore The glinting blade of Death so near his throat. I'll take you at your word. See. My sword's put up. We are no more at war.
TIRESIAS:	A futile gesture from a man afraid, To one who cannot see the kindly act.
OEDIPUS:	What riddle's this? What hermit's private jest?
TIRESIAS:	Look at my eyes, boy! Look at my eyes! Two eyes which shine with light, yet let none in.
OEDIPUS:	You're blind! Ha! No wonder Death holds little fear for you, You walk already through it's dark, cold, vales, And taste its hollow solitude each day. Forgive me my mistrust. No greater curse can haunt a living man, Than seeing not this world, where all is sight.
TIRESIAS:	You trust me now you know I cannot see?
OEDIPUS:	I do. And beg you to forgive my foolish pride.
TIRESIAS:	I do. And hope this righteous act is not your last, For in this way, you may, as time goes on, Find comfort, hope and peace from all your woes. But let's proceed. Recount your tale, the night is drawing in. These fleecy cloaks will keep our bodies warm,

But 'tis not wise to tempt this wind too much,
It cuts a man far deeper than your sword,
And chills the very marrow of his bones.

OEDIPUS: If you can bring some comfort to my pain,
You'll warm me more than any fleece could do,
And make this icy blast a summer's breeze.
And yet,
I hesitate to make my story known
To strangers newly met on this far hill,
But then,
If I do not this tale unburden soon,
I think my heart will rip my head apart,
And shake all sense of reason from my brain.
I'm tempest toss'd! A bark upon a sea,
That's whipped by fiery passions from within,
And dashed upon the rocks of heartless fate,
To rot forever on some unknown shore.
No human ear 'cept mine has heard my woe,
So listen while I make my terror known,
And do not judge too harshly of my life
For I am cursed by actions long ago,
Pertaining to my lineage and birth,
And I must suffer for my father's father's crimes
Yet never see my father's face again.

NILEUS: *(To Tiresias)* He raves like one insane.

TIRESIAS: *(To Nileus)* His past, although he blames his father's line,
Is laid up at his feet for him to bear,
Such horror would drive any man insane.
And yet,
We all must learn to live our lives like this,
Be conscious of the acts we choose to make,
For actions we perform in present time,
Dictate the type of future we attain,
While those we once enacted in the past,
Contribute to the state we now maintain.

OEDIPUS: Sit down,
I'll pace about some more,
These words need active movements to absolve.

               (pause)

               Like you, I've been to Delphi's sacred shrine,

103

(Encouraged there by Hippodamia's guile)
To seek an answer to a common lie
Made known about myself by some drunk fool.
When there, I soon obtained the right to plead,
And carried out the needful rituals due:
I purged myself, and bathed - as all must do -
Offered up libations; silent chants,
And shrived myself of all my former crimes.
This done, I made my way into that shrine,
That gilded chamber of the speaking voice,
Where man and god in mystery combine
To learn the hidden secrets of their fate.
A tripod-mounted throne filled up that room
And stood above a chasm dark and deep,
Which plunged into the very core of earth;
The sacred home of wisdom, life, and death.
A golden light emitted from those depths,
And played along the structure of that seat,
While incense clouds came wafting from that deep,
To fill the air with perfume soft and sweet,
And raise our mundane thoughts to thoughts divine.
A booming drum, like thunder, then rang out,
And whistles pierced the vibrant, pregnant air,
Heralding, to all who stood in fear,
The approach of Pythia, sage priestess of this sphere.
She swept into that room like one entranced,
And throwing off her robes and mystic crown,
Climbed onto that tripod-mounted throne,
And fell into a silent, senseless, swoon.
Then smoke of vibrant yellow filled our lungs,
Swirling from that chasm dark and deep,
That chasm, where Apollo's brittle voice,
Breaks ope' the mould of Time to mortal ears.
The room fell wholly silent as she sat,
Transfixed upon her throne like one long dead
Communing with the gods in soundless dread.
At last, she gasped for breath and ope'd her eyes,
And, bowing to the suppliants one by one,
Allowed the intercession to commence.
Being first, I stepped towards that sacred Sage,
And made obeisance due to her pure form,
Then kneeling down before that burning pyre,
I put my question to her - as one should -
To learn what truth Apollo might reveal.
But no!
Before the god could make his answer known,

A silent wind dipped out the burning flares,
Consumed in one vast sweep all radiant light,
And turned that glowing pyre to blackest night.
Then Pythia -
That living link between both man and god -
Wracked with wild contortions on the floor,
While sulphurous clouds consumed her twisted form,
And billowed like the waves of some great storm.
Her voice,
All gurgling, coughing, choked, and hoarse,
Cries out in one loud harsh, inhuman, wail,
A sound unfit for any living ear,
Which froze the silent watchers in their fear.
Two priest ran in, to hold her writhing frame,
While others sought to tend that sacred flame.
And she,
Oblivious to the panic in the room,
Began the stern pronouncement of my fate:
"Do not return to where you once were born.
For doom and foul destruction follow there.
Your father, you will slay with your own sword;
Your mother, take as wife to your own child."

(Tiresias stands)

TIRESIAS: Such ugly news. Her word and thought is clear.
              But offered she no light?

OEDIPUS: I know not, for I stayed to hear no more,
              For at that point I left that room and ran,
              Out into the swirling streets below,
              My heart amazed with horror at its fate.
              And then,
              As if I had not suffered pain enough,
              A band of soldiers, seeking for revenge,
              Set on me, and demanded that I fight,
              For they had served with Laius in the war,
              And thought this paltry peace no peace at all.
              Before I knew, my sword had been unsheathed,
              And I dispatched them all with swift, sure, blows,
              Then headed for the hills to nurse my woes.
              And when I saw you moving cross my path,
              Assumed you further rabble from the war,
              Come to lay an ambush on my head.

TIRESIAS: Poor wasted youth,

Your tale is one that no man wants to hear;
A catalogue heaped high with countless woes.
So full of horror is your life to date,
And heads towards a future filled with hate.
That all must feel great sorrow for your pain.

OEDIPUS: Your pity and your sadness touch me not!
I want some active answer to my plight,
Not some old fool's condolences and shame!
You spoke before of easing my wild storm,
Where is this hope, this comfort you made boast?
That is what I need, not rheumy eyes.

TIRESIAS: *(gently)* I spoke of comfort, hope, and peace from woe,
And these indeed I'll offer up to you,
But you must make some effort to absorb
The truth of all this pain that you've endured.

OEDIPUS: What truth is there in horror, tell me that?

TIRESIAS: Horror shapes our heart to bear the truth.
This Fate decreed; this Future prophesied;
Are truths about yourself that you must face,
In order that the power which they contain,
Can be dispersed and cause no further pain.

OEDIPUS: Riddles, jests and lies!
Why do you mountain hermits twist the truth,
And cloak your speech in such a foul disguise?

TIRESIAS: 'List well, then child,
I'll tell you something straight.
What you have seen and heard is but your life
Made conscious to the reason of your thought.
Reflect on what has passed,
And go no further till your mind has cleared.
These prophecies, this family curse you fear,
Are all but dark potential in yourself.
They are not acts that happen in the world,
But part of you.
Draw breath. Go find some quiet cave.
Renounce this hectic life and live with us.
I'll be your teacher, lead your mind to peace,
Burn out this ancient terror from your heart,
And help you to redress this weight of woe.

106

OEDIPUS: Ha!
             Is this your answer to the pain I feel,
             The torture and the terror I endure?
             You blind old fool! You give me nothing!
             Nothing, but the folly of your age!
             What good is sitting here above the world,
             When life is lived forever in the plains?
             Begone old man, before I end you here,
             And prove your source of comfort, hollow dreams!

TIRESIAS: Proud foolish man, then go down to your doom!
             I've set the facts before you, you must choose.
             No man controls another this you know,
             But think again before you make your move.
             Your fate is sealed, your actions-past, performed,
             Wound up like some great spring that will uncoil,
             And hurl you ever onward to your doom.
             Unless you heed my words and stay with me,
             All that the Delphic Oracle has spoke,
             Will haunt you like the echo haunts the voice,
             Which shouts its taunting message to the air.
             Think once again before you move to go,
             And do not rush so rashly to your tomb.

OEDIPUS: Bah! You weak pathetic fool!
             D'you, think I take these empty threats to heart?
             Shiver here and die.
             I leave you in your wilderness to rot.

             (*He begins to leave in the direction he came on.*)

TIRESIAS: (*shouts after him*) Beware of women, boy!
             The first one that you meet will seal your fate!

OEDIPUS: Beware your own delusions, foolish cur!

             (*Oedipus exits*)

NILEUS: Can we not help him, Sir?

TIRESIAS: No. He spurned our proffered help.

NILEUS: Then he is fated to the Oracle's cruel curse?

TIRESIAS: Indeed.

107

NILEUS: Oh then I pity him.
                 His future seems so tragic and unjust.

TIRESIAS: No boy no.
                 'Tis not unjust, but all that he deserves.
                 He's brought this fate about through his own deeds.
                 So never pity those who spurn your help.
                 To pity, is to do a man great harm,
                 And renders him no better than a beast,
                 Which lives to prove the toast at some dull feast.
                 A man who will not help himself is lost,
                 Until great Time's eternal wheel spins round,
                 And shows to him the folly of his ways.
                 Look over there, to yon far distant plain,
                 Are there not, some dark and dismal clouds,
                 That swirl in angry whorls above a town?

NILEUS: There are indeed.

TIRESIAS: Well that is Thebes, the place to which he's bound,
                 And those, no clouds, but emblems of his fate.
                 For he, made fully conscious of his acts,
                 Has chosen to ignore what he should do,
                 And takes up arms with Ignorance, and Hate,
                 To fight a loosing battle 'gainst his fate.
                 But come, let's take ourselves away,
                 This icy wind has cut too deep today.

                 (Exit Tiresias and Nileus.)

                 END OF ACT 2 SCENE 4

ACT 2 SCENE 5

Hippodamia's chambers

(*Enter the Watchman.*)

LIVIA: What draws you here?

WATCHMAN: I come to see the queen.

LIVIA: She cannot see you now.
Tis the moony time of month when blood runs free,
And women keep their counsel 'mongst themselves.

WATCHMAN: D'you think the sight of blood will wet my breeks?
I must impart my news to her at once.

LIVIA: No! She has not slept all week
And needs her strength to journey o'er to Thebes.
Call on her when her psyche's more robust.
Or tell your news to me.

WATCHMAN: No! It must be her. No other ear will do.

LIVIA: She is infirm and will not hear you now,
Call back some other time.

WATCHMAN: You filthy whore!
D'you think I come unmindful of her wrath,
Or fail to grasp the pain she must endure?
My news is such I must impart it now.

LIVIA: You are more agitated than I've seen,
And all your filthy lewdness has been curbed.
Your news must be of some import for this.
Yet you must wait. She will not see you now.

(*Enter Hippodamia in a white night gown. Looking pale and
wan.*)

HIPPODAMIA: What noise is this that draws me from my bed?
Oh 'tis you,
You foul mouthed creature from the sewer of Life.
What brings you here?

109

WATCHMAN: I bring bad news.

LIVIA: I've told him to be gone.

HIPPODAMIA: Fret not. I'll hear his ragged news.
               My recent loss has hardened me 'gainst pain.
               Go in and make fresh comfort of my bed.

               (*Exit Livia.*)

               Your news and make it brief.
               I have no time to waste on such as you.

WATCHMAN: My news is brief, but bad,
               And pains my tongue to pour it in your ears.

HIPPODAMIA: Pour on.
               These ears have lately filled with so much woe,
               I doubt your news can oust what's gone before.
               Has Chrysippus been killed?

WATCHMAN: Oh no! Not Chrysippus.
               Their court is full of Chrysippus,
               His name's on every tongue,
               Filling every mouth with sweet delight.
               Oh no, my news is not of Chrysippus.

HIPPODAMIA: [*aside*] Three months, and still he lives and breathes.
               This boy has tried my patience to the full.
               [*aloud*] This news was bad enough, is worse to come?

WATCHMAN: Aye. My worst is yet to come.
               After Laius signed the pact of peace...

HIPPODAMIA: You say the pact of peace is signed?

WATCHMAN: Aye. Three days ago.

HIPPODAMIA: Three days! Then you did see it done?

WATCHMAN: Indeed.
               Not only I, but hundreds saw it done.
               T'was witnessed by a crowd within his court
               That pushed and shoved like drunkards at a brawl,
               Cheering, shouting, screaming out their din;

And heaping so much praise upon their King,
That he could not but think he was divine.
Three times he did but falter to begin,
Three times their mindless paean drowned his speech:
And when his ring impressed his imprint home,
They raised their voice in one almighty roar,
That shook the very palace to the core.
But were you not informed this had been done?

HIPPODAMIA: That treaty is not due to bear his seal,
Until we reach his court tomorrow night.
[aside] This man usurps all pride and place of Kings.
That he should play the traitor to me now,
And rob me of my chance to reign supreme.
[aloud] Yet Chrysippus still lives?

WATCHMAN: Aye,
Alive and well, the favourite of his court.
And favourite of his bed if tales be true.

HIPPODAMIA: [aside] Laius shall suffer for this slight,
I will not let his passion rule my plans.
That boy must die, and Laius play his part,
Or he'll soon learn that treachery spells death.
[aloud] Your news, so far, is not what I would hear.
If your foul tongue did not still serve my ends,
I'd have your body tortured on the rack,
Until it was so broken and so bent,
Your present shape would seem Perfection's mould.

WATCHMAN: I only tell what these sharp senses see,
Not fit the story to the sweetest lie.
I warned you that my news was full of grief.

HIPPODAMIA: Then on if this be but preamble to your worst.

WATCHMAN: I dread to tempt your wrath,
For what I have to say you will not like.

HIPPODAMIA: I like not you, but give you space to breathe.

WATCHMAN: Would then some space for Lucien was found.

HIPPODAMIA: Lucien! What mean you by that jibe?
Why do you soil his name with your foul breath?

111

WATCHMAN: Because he has no breath to soil his own.
Lucien's dead!

HIPPODAMIA: Lucien. Dead?

WATCHMAN: Aye,
Laius skewered him through with his own sword.

HIPPODAMIA: Oh monstrous, vulgar villain of deceit!
That he should harm the flesh of one so dear.
How came he to this death?

WATCHMAN: T'was as I had begun,
After Laius signed that pact of peace,
We waited in a chamber near the throne,
For Lucien had made our purpose known
And craved a private audience with him.
At last he came, flamboyant and enflamed,
Puffed up with his good fortune and delight,
Like some Spring-Peacock showing off his tail.
At first his mood was courteous and kind,
Treating us with dignity and grace,
Till Lucien withdrew your sealed address
(The meat of which I've yet to ascertain)
And handed it to him, with much aplomb.
He read it like a man condemned to death,
And all at once the blood drained from his face,
As if some leech had sucked his body dry.
He stuttered, stammered, choked at every word,
Then fury rose to flush his cheeks once more.
He roars aloud:-
"Vain harlot of Ambition's greedy lust,
No harm shall come to him, whom now I love."
Cursing loud your name, as if an oath,
He swoops upon poor Lucien, like a hawk,
Tearing him to shreds with hands and nails.
In self-defence did Lucien draw his sword,
But Laius quickly wrest it from his grasp,
And stabs him six-times over, through the chest.
As Lucien fell, that furied fiend cries out:-
"Take this as answer to that harlot's curse!"
And in one sweep deprives him of his head.
Then, holding it aloft for all to see,
Commands me, in a voice not of this earth,
"Go, tell your ugly mistress that I say,
My peace is made with Pelops' only son,

And all our former bargains are revoked."
Then thrusting this poor bloody ball at me
Demanded that I bring it here to you.

(*He presents a head wrapped in a bloody cloth.*)

HIPPODAMIA: Ahh!!
Sweet father of my child. Oh Lucien! My lovely Lucien.
That you should be so cruelly, chopped and changed.
Give that to me!

(*she takes the head*)

Oh hapless, headless, youth.
Decapitated, dead, and drained of life.
To be so cruelly butchered by that fiend.

WATCHMAN: Oh mistress.
Let me bring you comfort. Ease your pain.

HIPPODAMIA: Begone you varlet! Bringer of bad news!
Crawl back into some orifice of hell,
And never let me see your face again.

WATCHMAN: I...I...

HIPPODAMIA: Begone!

(*Exit Watchman, slowly, pitifully.*)

HIPPODAMIA: Oh Lucien. My lovely Lucien. I will not let you die.
I'll breathe again fresh breath into your lips.

(*She slowly unwraps the head.*)

Oh! Sweet youthful face, wipe off this crusted blood,
Which should not stain the whiteness of your brow.
Oh come not mists, you cloud me in this task,
And fill my eyes with sights they should not see.
Begone!

(*She flails her hands about dispersing an imaginary mist.*)

See how his eyes stare wildly into mine,
As if his heart still burnt with tender love.
Oh father, do not weep those tears for me,

I'll keep you safe. Return you to your throne,
And never let that poison touch your lips.
Oh had I but the strength to alter time,
I'd wipe away the sorrows from your brow,
Bring back to life the sallow of your cheeks,
Draw forth your breath and live with you in peace.
But hark!
My baby cries. It has my father's face.
And carries on his line through its young form.
Tush. Tush.
Your mama will not let you come to harm.

(*She holds it up to the sky.*)

This third born child will wear the royal crown,
Exalt our race and purge our family name.
But look. 'Tis dead.
It shrinks within the hollow of my womb.
Oh father! Father! Take not such revenge.
Begone vile sight! I will not see you more!
Peeweet! Peeweet!
What birds are these that lure me from my nest?
Peeweet! Peeweet!
'Tis lapwings singing. Hear their joyful tune.
Peeweet! Peeweet!
Their voices cry for one who sleeps too long.
Rise up. Rise up. They will not let us sleep.
We will go hunting pheasants in the dawn,
And bring back pretty feathers for our caps.
Peeweet! Peeweet!
See how they wrap their wings around their young,
And give them comfort with their lulling tongues.
Peeweet! Peeweet!
They draw me to your fireside once more.

(*Livia rushes in followed by Watchman.*)

LIVIA: Quickly 'fore the madness takes full hold.
                Mistress, distress yourself no more
                Let me relieve you of that bloody sight.

HIPPODAMIA: Tread gentle daughter, 'tis your father fast asleep.

WATCHMAN: What words are these she says?

LIVIA: [*To Watchman*] 'Tis a fever grips her spirit. Pay no heed.

114

What a fool you were to let her see this sight.
As if she has not suffered woes enough.
Go. Bring in those herbs.

(He exits.)

Your majesty 'tis I, Livia.

HIPPODAMIA: Livia? That name has no place here.
Peeweet! Peeweet! They lure me from my nest.
And try to stop my offspring win the crown.

(Livia tries to remove the head. They struggle.)

I will not let them help to lay you down.

LIVIA: Your majesty! Come to! Shake out of this!

(She slaps her.)

HIPPODAMIA: Oh do not strike me sire, I meant no harm.
It was but poison in an empty cup,
Your greedy dogs in hunger lapped it up.

LIVIA: Shake out! Come to! Fight off this horrid curse.

(She shakes her vigorously and slaps her again).

HIPPODAMIA: Livia! What insult happens here?

LIVIA: You have been dreaming.

(R*e-enter the Watchman.)*

Give me those herbs! And fetch your queen a chair!
Here mistress, ease you pain.

HIPPODAMIA: I feel a chill descending on my bones.
Why do I feel so cold?

LIVIA: 'Tis but the air.
Sit silent for a while and close your eyes,
This soothing balm will warm you by and by.
[*To Watchman*] Begone. You've caused enough distress.

HIPPODAMIA: Oh! Woe is me!

WATCHMAN: This sigh would cause the hardest heart to break.

LIVIA: Begone. She'll presently revive,
               And will not wish to see the likes of you.
               Take in that filthy curse and leave at once!
               And not a word of this to any ear.

               (*The Watchman exits slowly with the head.*)

HIPPODAMIA: Oh Livia, am I infirm?
               What's happened here? My mind is all distraught.

LIVIA: T'was fever mam. You were o'ercome with grief.

HIPPODAMIA: I have more grief to bear than all mankind,
               And were I not so righteous in my cause,
               This heart would break and spill my sorrows out.

LIVIA: Then galvanize your heart 'gainst one more blow.
               Poor Lucien is dead.

HIPPODAMIA: Dead? Lucien dead? Laius!
               Oh Lucien!
               To be so cruelly butchered by that fiend.
               I'll scream for vengeance to the highest gods,
               And wreak revenge on all his hapless state.
               That king will taste the furies of my mind,
               That he should rob sweet Lucien of his life.
               Go Livia,
               Search out those deadly potions I have brewed,
               And store them in a phial that will not break.
               Tomorrow night King Laius will eat well,
               And taste my hidden wrath with every bite.
               Come I'll help you to this task. (*she faints.*)

LIVIA: Guards! Guards!
               Poor wretched soul.
               Her hatred and her sorrow both contend,
               To win control o'er her poor, restless heart.
               She has so many roles that she must play,
               She cannot tell what's fantasy or fact.

               (*Enter some Guards.*)

               She was o'er come. Convey her to her bed,

116

Where she may sleep and soothe her o'erwrought head.

(*They carry her off, followed by Livia.*)

END OF ACT 2 SCENE 5

ACT 2 SCENE 6

A vegetable garden in the court of King Laius. Enter Lambrus carrying a spade and Pitheus carrying a sack.

LAMBRUS: Come Pitheus, keep up. Keep up.
We must not fail our master in this task.
They say King Pelops and his Noble Queen will grace our royal court tomorrow night
and we must baste the meat which they will eat.

PITHEUS: We'll baste it well, for we are great basters.

LAMBRUS: Indeed we are. Indeed we are. There are not many who can baste like me.

(he uses the spade to make basting actions)

I am the King of basters. Why, that's meet, The king of basters.
I like that. My basting is boasted far and wide.

PITHEUS: Far and wide. Far and wide.

LAMBRUS: Aye, far and wide. Tis true. But come. Let's gather up a great herd of wild garlic
for tomorrow's feast.

PITHEUS: Aye let's. *(declaiming)* A great multitudinous herd incarcerate.

LAMBRUS: *(mimicking him)* 'A great multitudinous herd incarcerate?' What stuff is this?

PITHEUS: Why, 'tis a speech.

LAMBRUS: A speech?

PITHEUS: Aye. A speech from a Stroller's play.

LAMBRUS: A speech from a Stroller's play? 'A great multitudinous herd incarcerate.'

It sounds more like the burble of a fool.

118

PITHEUS: Oh no. 'Tis an acting speech, acted by the man who was the queen.

LAMBRUS: The man who was the queen? 'Tis tinker's twaddle and deserves the whip.

                    (*he makes to strike him*)

PITHEUS: No. No. I beg you. Some player from the court did last night act this speech before the King.

LAMBRUS: The King you say?

PITHEUS: Aye.

LAMBRUS: Why. Then 'tis a good speech. A fine speech. The very model of a speech. You know it well?

PITHEUS: Indeed I do. It filled my heart with such a lofty sentinel that I did commit it to my memory at once,
                    in order that I might reprove it again and again.

LAMBRUS: Then you did well to do so.
                    For what moves one to lofty sentinels is worthy of reproving.
                    Come, acquaint me with the meaning of it that I might rehearse
          a line or two.

PITHEUS: The meaning? Oh! I know not what it means. I did but learn the words.

LAMBRUS: You know not what it means!
                    Then thou art not but a proper ass to commit to memory words,
          the meaning of which,
                    you do not reprehend.

PITHEUS: Oh, but I did reprehend them then, tis now I have forgot.

LAMBRUS: Then you are a buffoon to forget that which you did not even know.

                    Why, if all the world did that, we'd soon forget our left hand
          (*holds up his right*)
                    from our right!

                    (*Holds up his left - Pitheus looks puzzled,
                    and tries to work it out on his hands*)

119

Come, play the speech that I may find the meaning for myself.

PITHEUS: "Out Out, you great sea multitudinous incarcerate!"
"Will never soap wash out this stink of death?"
"Farewell I must away."
Think you it not meet?

LAMBRUS: "Out Out". Mmn. Tis meet indeed, and lofty in its sentinel. But is that all?

PITHEUS: All?

LAMBRUS: Aye. Is that all the speech?

PITHEUS: Oh no, Twas a long speech. A very long speech. An exceedingly long speech.

LAMBRUS: Then where is all the rest?

PITHEUS: The rest? The rest? Why, that is in the betrayal of it.
This bit here; "Out Out, you great sea multitudinous incarcerate!"
this is the beginning, where the queen comes on, or the man who played the queen,
for you must know it was not the real queen.

LAMBRUS: I knew it would not be the real queen, her mood is far too sultry for this part.

PITHEUS: (*annoyed at the interruption*) And this bit "Farewell I must away." brings up the end, where she must leave.

LAMBRUS: Yes, yes, I took that for the case, but what about the other bits between?

PITHEUS: The other bits between?

LAMBRUS: Aye. The other bits between. (*long pause*) Well?

PITHEUS: (*sheepishly*) The other bits between I have forgot.

LAMBRUS: Forgot! Forgot! You said you had committed it to heart.

PITHEUS: (*indignant*) I had! I did! I have not forgot the bits I did remember.

Tis the bits I did forget that I've forgot.

LAMBRUS: Forget! Forgot! Why this is poor. You cannot say a speech with all the rest forgot.

PITHEUS: You can. You can. The other bits are acting and need not words to show them.

It is all in the betrayal. Watch:-
"Out Out, you great sea multitudinous incarcerate!"
"Will never soap wash out this stink of death?"
Then comes the acting part, watch how I betray it.

(*he walks about holding his nose making out there is an awful smell*)

Then comes a wailing and a beating of breasts like so. (*he beats his breasts*)
"Oh!" Oh!" "Ah!" (*he stops*)

LAMBRUS: And then?

PITHEUS: And then, (*quickly*) some bits I have forgot, and then:-
"Farewell I must away." (*he waves his hands vigorously*)

LAMBRUS: No. No. 'Tis marred. 'Tis marred.

PITHEUS: Marred?

LAMBRUS: Aye, your deliverance mars it. You are not a pretty player. Not one whit a pretty player.

PITHEUS: (*shakes his head sadly*) Not a pretty player. Not one whit a pretty player.

LAMBRUS: Behold. I'll show you how to carry off this role. I have a natural talent for this art.

E'en though we only have but half the speech. (*he recites with great gusto*)
"Out Out, you great sea multitudinous incarcerate!"
"Will never soap wash out this stink of death?"
"Farewell I must away."
See the way I draw the sentinel out of it. The stretching of my arm. The pointing of my chin towards the crowd.

PITHEUS: (*looking about*) Crowd? What crowd? We are alone.

LAMBRUS: Why the crowd that is the audience you fool!

121

PITHEUS: I see no crowd.

LAMBRUS: There is no crowd, tis all up here. Imagination. You must
imagine there is a crowd.
            Look, this patch of garlic is the stage, yonder is the theatre with
        its crowd,
                and I am the great actor holding forth.
                Watch how I highlight all the tiny nuisance of it.

                (*he recites again with even greater gusto*)

                "Out Out, you great sea multitudinous incarcerate!"
                "Will never soap wash out this stink of death?"
                "Farewell I must away."
                Note you not the nuisance that I make?

PITHEUS: Oh indeed, indeed. Bravo! Bravo! Why 'tis like the real thing.
                A very great nuisance you have made of it. Very great indeed.

LAMBRUS: The crowd adore me. (*he bows*)

                (P*itheus looks about for the crowd very suspiciously but says
                nothing.*)

PITHEUS: Shall we gather up some garlic for the feast?

LAMBRUS: No. No. I'll play the part again. This acting suits me well. Sit
you there.
                Be you all the ample audience of Greece.
                Why that's meet think you not, 'all the ample audience of
        Greece'. I like that.
                 I'll add it to the speech. Sit you there and be you the crowd.
                Play it like an audience in court:- rattle your jewels; cough and
        splutter;
                clear your throat in the silent parts; rustle papers when I pause
        for breath,
                and generally distract your time away, until you vent your fury
        in applause.
                Can you fill this part?

PITHEUS: I'll try. (*he sits*)

LAMBRUS: Good. (*he composes himself*) "Out out..."

PITHEUS: (*Pitheus begins to applaud loudly*) More! More! Bravo! Bravo!

LAMBRUS: Not yet! Not yet! Be silent till I bow.

PITHEUS: I was rehearsing.

LAMBRUS: Rehearsing! Rehearsing! You do not need rehearsing for your
part.

PITHEUS: Oh but 'twill be better if I do.

LAMBRUS: No. No. Your part needs no rehearsing. 'Tis I who must
rehearse.

      bow.
           Sit silent while I start again, and do not shout for more until I

           "Out, Out, ye ample audience..."

           (*Enter Laius & Chrysippus*)

PITHEUS: Lambrus! Lambrus! Oh Lambrus.

LAMBRUS: Not now. Not now, I'm in my role. (*he starts again*)
           "Out Out... you ample audience of Greece,
           You great sea multitudinous incarcerate!
           Will never soap wash out this stink of death?
           Oh. Oh. Oh. I am undone.
           Farewell I must away. (*he bows*)

LAIUS: Bravo! Bravo!
           Is not this inspired nonsense, Chrysippus?

CHRYSIPPUS: It seems so sir, and yet he plays it well.
           And shows a certain vigour in his part.

           (*Lambrus continues to bow*)

LAIUS: Bravo sir! Bravo!

LAMBRUS: Oh your majesty. I did not see you come.
           I thought you were the audience of Greece.

           (*he stares daggers at Pitheus*)

LAIUS: What! You want the whole of Greece?
           Is one mere King not audience enough?

LAMBRUS: Oh No. No.

You are perfect ample audience indeed.

PITHEUS: Aye. Perfectly ample.
             Much better than this crowd who stand and watch.

LAIUS: Crowd? There is no crowd!
             What mischief occupies you scoundrels now?

PITHEUS: We gather garlic for tomorrow's feast.

LAIUS: You gather garlic, by reciting words!
             What ancient form of sorcery is this?

PITHEUS: None. None.

LAMBRUS: (*pushing Pitheus aside*) Why, that is right.
             Your majesty has guessed the matter right.
             An ancient form of sorcery it is.
             This garlic is most stubborn to be off,
             And clings and clings and will not loose its grip,
             Until I must recite this magic verse,
             And charm it off the stem with these rough words.

LAIUS: You charm it off the stem with these rough words?
             You are a proper rogue,
             And will prate whatever nonsense takes your tongue.
             Get you indoors, attend some other task
             And leave this garlic to the gardener's hand.

PITHEUS: Oh do not beat us sir. We meant no harm.
             This is the play t'was acted yesternight,
             And we reprove it in our simple way
             That we might gain its lofty sentinels.

LAIUS: You reprove it, to gain its sentinels?
             I think I do not wish to hear much more.
             Go! Go! Go put your own art to the test,
             And leave the Strolling players free to theirs.

PITHEUS: We will. We will.
             We'll bake some pretty sweet-meats for the feast.

LAMBRUS: Aye, sweet-meats that will terrorize your tongue,
             And give you such sweet tastes you'll cry for more.

LAIUS: Terrorize my tongue? Begone! I will not sanction more!

124

(*Exit Lambrus and Pitheus running.*)

Oh Chrysippus!
Why do I gladly tolerate such fools,
When all they do is mock me to my face?

CHRYSIPPUS: Oh do not rail them so,
Your fondness for them, countermands your ire,
And shows you but a traitor to your tongue.

LAIUS: Tis true,
I hold their folly fondly in my heart.
But yet, are they not foolish to a fault,
And needy of Correction's angry rod?

CHRYSIPPUS: They may be foolish, but their hearts are pure,
And act more out of kindness, than contempt.
They are but wayward children, lost and scared.
Be tolerant and patient of their faults,
For they have not the sense to help themselves.

LAIUS: Oh dear, sweet, Chrysippus,
You will not see another creature harmed,
Nor hear a bad word said 'gainst any man,
Regardless of the nature of his crimes.
You are the kindest, gentlest thing alive,
And shower your boundless love o'er all mankind.
Oh how my life has changed since knowing you:
My kingdom grown to peace; my people free;
My land, so long lain barren by this war,
Is blessed with such fecundity and hope,
That boughs bend down, o'er laden with fresh fruit,
And farmers cannot harvest all they sow.
The very air smells sweeter since you came,
As if your gentle breath, perfumed the wind,
And blew the scent of love in every face.
Oh Chrysippus,
You bring such comfort to this ancient heart,
I feel like some quaint, tongue-tied, lisping youth,
Who stutters at the very sight of Love.

CHRYSIPPUS: Your eloquence belies the role it pleads.

LAIUS: Oh do not mock me in my flights of joy,
Love's poetry is full of such conceits.

125

CHRYSIPPUS: Oh Laius, I do not mock you,
              But spoke without due thought.
              Forgive me, for my mind was crossed with hate.

LAIUS: Your mind was crossed with hate? Why this is strange,
              You are not prone to bouts of angry thought.
              What is it that distracts you in this way?

CHRYSIPPUS: Oh. Some phantom from the past.
              My mind was on this feast tomorrow night,
              And fearful lest some ugliness befell.
              I know that evil woman means me harm,
              And find myself contracted by my fear -
              Caught up, constricted, wrapped within myself -
              And petrified that I might cease to be,
              Before I have accomplished all I may.

LAIUS: What's this? Shake off these sapping doubts.
              You have no need to fear that wretched hag.
              Will I not see she does not do you harm?

CHRYSIPPUS: No doubt you will, but yet, I fear her still.
              Her image haunts my thinking every day,
              And rises like some dark, ungainly blot,
              To stain what little goodness I attain.

LAIUS: Oh Chrysippus, no more!
              Your goodness overflows in all you do,
              And is a perfect standard for us all.
              How can this 'royal' whore, compare with you?

CHRYSIPPUS: I oft times think my talk of love and peace,
              Is but the misplaced fear of my own fear,
              And hides like raging violence in my breast,
              Tearing at the fabric of my being.
              Oh would that I could find within myself,
              The strength to draw these feelings into light,
              Expose them for the weakness that they are,
              And cast their cribbing, confines to the air.

LAIUS: Oh say not so.
              You are the gentlest creature on this earth,
              So pure, so kind, so perfect in your ways,
              That words cannot express your godlike charms.

126

Do not despise the qualities you have,
But revel in the wonder of yourself,
And cast these hazy phantoms from your mind.

CHRYSIPPUS: Oh Laius, I thank you for your praise,
But praise will not relieve these pangs of pain.
Oh why did Hippodamia choose to come?

LAIUS: She must, your father wished it so,
And we must show her courtesy and grace.
For as you know, he's blind to all her faults,
And sees her as a true and loving wife.
But have no fear, she will not do you harm
This arm would gladly speed her into hell,
Were not it for the fact that she's His queen.
She will be closely followed through the court
And every move she makes made know to me,
Take comfort in these facts and shed your fear.
This feast will pass off quickly, serve its end,
A show of peaceful friendship 'tween our courts –
And they will be departed 'fore the dawn.
Bear up, she will not have her way.
In politics we oft must act, and seem,
What in our daily life would be a lie.
Your duty as a prince demands you smile,
E'en though your thoughts be scowling all the while.
Do this for me,
And think it but a favour for your friend.
T'will soon be o'er,
A small discomfort for a lifetime's ease.
What say you to this plan?

CHRYSIPPUS: I think I'd rather die than play this role,
For Truth is far more noble than a lie.
And yet, I'll play the part,
For this deception, though it pains my heart,
Brings happiness to greater hearts than mine,
And I must serve both kingdoms how I may.

LAIUS: Bravo young sir and spoken like a prince.

CHRYSIPPUS: Yet I have thoughts whose coming draws dark clouds,
O'er all the golden sunshine of my mind.
Some haunting premonition of dark deeds,
Which even now, speed quickly to their end.
But let's go in,

127

I dwell upon this ugliness too much,
And grace her with more hate than she deserves.

LAIUS: Oh Chrysippus,
                But you alone could love that woman now,
                Knowing what she tried to have me do.
                Come,
                If you could teach but half the world your love,
                Mankind would soon outshine the gods above.

                (*Exit Laius with his arm around Chrysippus fondly*)

                    END OF ACT 2 SCENE 6

ACT 2 SCENE 7

The court of King Pelops.

(*Pelops is walking up and down in Hippodamia's antechamber very slowly, he eyes the wall that keeps her from him. he looks exhausted, dishevelled, and worried.*)

PELOPS: This room is cold. The whole place reeks of death,
And shadows from the night now haunt my days.
Is this the world that she and I desired?
Is this the world our marriage bed devised?

(*Livia enters.*)

Ah! Livia!
How is my gentle queen? May I approach her yet?

LIVIA: She's sleeping sound and should not be disturbed.
And does not wish to see you 'till she's well.
Lest you are overcome by her pale sight.

PELOPS: Am I to be denied her yet again?

LIVIA: Be silent sir. You'll draw her from her sleep.

PELOPS: Oh why has she been blighted with this curse,
As if we have not suffered pain enough?
This month has been a torment without end;
Her screaming voice has seared my sleepless nights,
Drawing forth dread spectres from my brain,
And filling all my dreams with sights from hell!

LIVIA: Good sir do not disburden here.
This day has run too long for human care,
And burdened me with more than I can bear.
I have no strength to share your heavy load,
Nor add your heap of sorrows to my own.

PELOPS: This needs must out! I'll go insane,
If I can't voice the horror of my pain.
I have no other ears but yours to tell,
Save these I own,
Who know this wretched story word for word.

LIVIA: Then do your worst,
                I think 'twill seem but light and fresh relief,
                Compared to all that's happened here today.

PELOPS: Tis dreams, tis hate-filled, hellish dreams,
                That cut me to the quick and sap all hope.
                Each night, three apparitions haunt mine eyes,
                As if, strange premonitions of dark deeds,
                Sent here to leech the sanity from thought!
                The first, my former wife - arrayed in gold -
                And shrouded in a veil of glowing mist,
                Beckons me to join her in her tomb,
                Where comfort and sweet loving seem to lie.
                But as I move to join her, she recedes,
                Plucked up into the arms of some foul fiend,
                And whisked away to some un-lighted realm.
                Then Chrysippus - long parted from our shore -
                Stands silent in the darkness of that gloom,
                Responding to the horror of this scene,
                By mouthing soundless screams of ceaseless pain,
                Which seem to rend all feeling from my brain.
                The third, more dreadful yet does then appear,
                As Lucien - a headless, ghoulish, wraith -
                Who motions me with arms of flailing light,
                To fly this court and leave my Queen to die,
                Desert her in the hour of her most need
                As if she was the cause of his demise!
                Each night these silent phantoms grow in strength,
                Until I do not dare to shut my eyes,
                Lest I am lost forever in this hell!
                And this, all this,
                Arising from the anguish of my Queen,
                Whom I am not at liberty to see!
                Oh Livia, advise me of her state,
                For I am driven mad with all this fright.

LIVIA: Please sir. No more!
                This is no place to catalogue your fears.
                We all have lived through horror these past weeks.
                You must have patience 'till her frailty goes.

PELOPS: Patience!
                I have no more of patience left to give.
                The shadow of her illness plagues my court,
                And casts perpetual darkness o'er my mood.

130

As if this war, which ravished us without,
Now turns to wreak its havoc from within!
These walls that separate us seem so frail,
But this long month have proved a flawless dam,
Holding back her anguish and her pain.
Yet I still feel her presence all around
Raising murky floods that smash this frame,
And gather like a tempest's fiery rage,
To crash upon our heads when we're asleep,
And drown us in our nature's deepest fears.

LIVIA: Do not go on! I cannot bear much more!
Have I not been beside her these long nights
Been witness to the suf'ring she's endured
And party to the terror of her sights?
'Tis ten o'clock, and I am fit for bed,
And do not have the strength to tend your needs.
Why should I bear the brunt of other's deeds,
And feel responsibility for all?
Get you inside.
Go play some gentle music for your nerves,
And put your strained appearance back to rights.
She would not wish to see you in this state.

PELOPS: Oh Livia, I think my heart will break,
For I am driven mad with all this fright
And cannot bear the thought that she might die.

LIVIA: She will not die. The fever's left her brain
And she'll regain her strength before the dawn.

PELOPS: Oh pray that it is so,
For Death has raped our country for so long
He knows not when to cease his senseless cull.
These wretched, sweat-soaked, nights have kindled fears
That some unkind divine is on our trail,
Intent to make a graveyard of our court.
She must not die! I could not bear such loss.
Two wives within the space of four short years.
'Tis more than my poor heart could entertain.

LIVIA: She will not die. But sleeps a healing sleep,
That nourishes with rest, and peaceful dreams.
She's suffered but a slight and short relapse
Through rising from her bed before due time.
Tomorrow, you will see her, fit and well.

PELOPS: We must to Thebes tomorrow, to my son.
             Will she be well for that?

LIVIA: I think she would not miss it for the world.
             Her costume has been set aside for days.
             And her two sons, advised to be on hand,
             To help her make this journey to that land.

PELOPS: Then let her sleep. And pray that she is well.
             The journey will be hard, and cost her much,
             I'll see we travel slowly through the day,
             With many stops, for rest, along the way.
             She should be with me when I sign that pledge,
             'Tis fitting and demanded of our state.
             Let's pray she has the strength to fill that role.
             But Livia, I need your help.
             I have some words to say,
             Yet do not know quite how they should be put?

LIVIA: Then tell me, sir, I'll help you if I can.
             But make it brief,
             The sands of night are running into day.

PELOPS: I worry 'bout her sons,
             And wish that they would stay here in our court,
             Not make this lengthy journey o'er to Thebes.
             They oft times cause effrontery and shame,
             And I cannot control their youthful ways.
             It would not do to jeopardize this peace,
             Which we, through much exertion, have achieved.
             Can you convey this gently when she wakes?
             She will not take it kindly, this I know,
             But we will make more speed if they remain,
             And I shall feel more confident and sure,
             That all will go according to the plan.

LIVIA: I'll tell her what you've said.

PELOPS: Good.
             I worry o'er the outcome of this trip,
             And wish that she was here to give me strength.
             I cannot rule forever on my own!
             Oh wretched age, and dull affairs of state,
             I would that they were gone, and I was free.
             Young Chrysippus must take my place 'fore long,

132

	For I grow weary of the constant fray,

For I grow weary of the constant fray,
That politics and Kingship does demand.
Attend your mistress well,
Convince her of the sense of what I say,
And pray that she is better 'fore the dawn,
For this is all too much for me alone.

LIVIA: I'll pray.
            And will convey the gist of your concern.

PELOPS: Good. Good. I'll leave you now,
            I have some further business to attend.
            We start at dawn. I'll greet her when she wakes,
            And we shall ride together through Thebes' gates.

            (*Exit Pelops slowly.*)

LIVIA: (*shakes her head*) You poor old man.
            You could not speak worse tidings if you tried.
            She will not like one jot of what you've said,
            Nor let her noble sons remain behind.
            How little you must know her scheming mind,
            Or any of the actions of this court.
            What pawns the mighty seem to those who share,
            The secrets of their human woes and care.
            But hold,
            My eyes no longer view this world aright
            This day has run full circle into night.
            Come Sleep, and put this world to flight,
            By soothing me in your soft dreamy light.

            (*exit Livia*)

            END OF ACT 2 SCENE 7

            END OF ACT TWO

133

ACT 3 SCENE 1

A chamber in the court of King Laius. Enter Oedipus disguised as a leper in a heavy black cloak with a hood, he approaches a Servant.

SERVANT: *(Harsh)* Keep back, leper!
Step no further forward than that line.
What brings you here? What is it you desire?

OEDIPUS: I come to see Prince Chrysippus.
I've heard he has the power to cure my kind.

SERVANT: Huh! Prince Chrysippus?
[aside] What fools these old men are.
[aloud] You want his magic touch to cure your ills?

OEDIPUS: I do.
Tis said his very breath is like a balm.

SERVANT: *[aside]* How gullible the old and sick become!
This boy has brought more nonsense to our court,
Than all the fools in Greece could ever dream.
[aloud] Wait here old man, he'll pass this way 'fore long,
He's been to pay his homage to the shrine,
And no doubt, brings forth blessings from the gods.
You know his face?

OEDIPUS: Only too well.

SERVANT: Good. Then I'll withdraw. Farewell.

(Exit Servant, shaking his head in amusement.)

OEDIPUS: Farewell. Oh how I long for "Welcome back".
Dear Chrysippus, do not desert me now,
I need some comfort from this endless hell.
I come, a lowly leper to this court,
Disguised like Death, for all my life seems death!
Dead friends; Dead hope; dead parents by this curse.
Oh would that Delphi's oracle ne'r spoke
Then I, at least, in ignorance could dwell,
Oblivious to the fate I must endure!
Oh Chrysippus,

Will you reject me like you did before,
Or help me share the horror I now know?

(Chrysippus approaches and crosses the stage.)

But look! He comes. Oh what a soothing sight.
I had forgot the beauty of your face.
How like that mystic vision he appears -
A creature too delightful for this earth.
But patience Praise, I'll play this lowly part,
Till I can ascertain where his love lies.
Hold there boy! Give ear to an old man's tongue?

(He limps forward.)

CHRYSIPPUS: Gladly sir. What would you have me hear;
Though judging by the heavy cloak you wear,
And all the painful slowness of your limp,
Twill be a tale replete with ample woe?

OEDIPUS: My tale is full of woe, as is my life,
And this - my leper's cloak -
Guards me 'gainst the fierceness of the sun,
Whose light makes itchy scabs of all my flesh,
And tears the very fabric of my skin.
My limp is but a legacy from birth,
And will be gone when I have taken rest.
But this is not the tale I'd have you hear.
It touches on another's heart - not mine.
List' well:-
I've travelled far, o'er mountains, vales and streams,
In search of one who was a loving friend.
And in my aged infirmity I come
To look for him in Thebes,
Where I have heard, he lately was espied.

CHRYSIPPUS: Then rest awhile, I'll bathe your tired feet,
And bring you comfort while your tale unfolds.

OEDIPUS: You'd bathe a leper's feet?

CHRYSIPPUS: Gladly sir.
If such a simple act might ease your pain.

OEDIPUS: No. Unhand me. Do not do that!
I would not have you soil yourself for me!
[*aside*] Oh Chrysippus,

135

Your kindness overflows all human bounds.
To bathe a leper's feet! What selfless love!
Oh what clear hope this action gives my heart.

CHRYSIPPUS: Have I done wrong? Why do you turn away?

OEDIPUS: You've done no wrong.
My heart has broken at your tender touch.
Too long I've shared my sorrow all alone,
Forgetting there was goodness in this world.
Although you cannot see, for my dark hood,
Your kindness has unlocked my salty tears,
Which even now run wetly down my cheeks.
I turned my head away,
For 'tis not manly to be seen to cry.
E'en though our feelings oft times wish it so.

CHRYSIPPUS: Come, flood the world with tears,
I'll not think any less of you for that.
They are not men who fear to shed their tears.

OEDIPUS: I am o'ercome.
If you can show such kindness to a cur,
What tenderness reserve you for your friends?

CHRYSIPPUS: I see no cur, nor should you think you're such.
I treat all men as equal in my heart,
Believing all mankind should do the same.
But come, tell me of your friend,
For though I'm not a native of this court,
I may know those who'll help you seek him out.

OEDIPUS: He was a youth who valued valiant sport,
Who diced with death and braved the battle's roar.
Yet held his friends most highly in his heart,
Pursuing gentle arts with equal care.
But lately - so I've heard - his life has changed,
For Fate has marked him out for endless woe,
And he now lives, a shadow of himself,
Encloaked in Horror's darkness and despair.

CHRYSIPPUS: What caused this change in one so strong and true?

OEDIPUS: Some curse that so unjustly haunts his name.
But tell me, will you help me seek him out?

136

CHRYSIPPUS: Indeed I shall.
               For such a friend deserves your kind support.
               Has he a name that we may know him by?

OEDIPUS: His name was Oedipus; Polybus' son.

CHRYSIPPUS: Oedipus!

OEDIPUS: You know the name?

CHRYSIPPUS: I know the man as well. You say he's here in Thebes?

OEDIPUS: So rumour goes.
               He was despised by those in Pelop's court,
               And sheltered here to 'scape their senseless ire.

CHRYSIPPUS: Despised? That is not true!
               He was a hero in my father's ranks,
               A Captain, and companion to myself.
               He never was despised.

OEDIPUS: Then you still hold him fondly in your heart?

CHRYSIPPUS: Indeed I do
               He was a loving friend who shared my thoughts,
               A good companion in my lonely hours,
               And I have sorely missed him these past months.
               For like yourself I know not where he is.
               He vanished from our court without farewell,
               And I have heard but rumours of his death
               Until your words rekindled my lost hope.

OEDIPUS: Then you will help me find where he is hid?

CHRYSIPPUS: Gladly.
               The knowledge that he's safe has thrilled my heart,
               Revived those happy mem'ries of our love.
               Oh how I long to see his smiling face,
               I would that he was with us even now!

OEDIPUS: He is! Here before your eyes!

               (He *throws off the hood to reveal his face.*)

CHRYSIPPUS: Oedipus.

OEDIPUS: Chrysippus. (*They embrace.*)

CHRYSIPPUS: Oh Oedipus, where have you been?
                I've missed you these past months,
                And why have you assumed this dark disguise?

OEDIPUS: I come disguised like this for my own good.
                For since I saw you last dark deeds have dogged my days,
                And made my life a hell beyond compare.
                I show the world an old and beaten man,
                Reflecting through this garb my inner woe.

CHRYSIPPUS: Oh Oedipus,
                What deeds have made you don this ugly cloak,
                That casts so dark a shadow o'er your world?
                You were so zestful, bright and full of life,
                What's killed the happy, vibrance of your youth?

OEDIPUS: You heard the rumours 'bout my doubtful birth,
                That ran with raucous fury round our camp?

CHRYSIPPUS: I did,
                But gave them no more thought than they deserved.

OEDIPUS: But I did not. My birth; my lineage; my life;
                Played upon my mind like carrion crows,
                Until they picked my wits clean from my brain.
                Then Hippodamia, who heard these rumours too,
                Suggested I depart to Delphi's shrine,
                To gain some true perspective on those lies.
                I left at once,
                Leaving her the charge of my farewells,
                And trusting her to pass my love to you.

CHRYSIPPUS: Her lips were loudly silent on this fact,
                And gave instead harsh broadcast of your faults,
                Which painted you a coward to our court.

OEDIPUS: Chameleon'd cur!
                She shows the colours that she thinks suit best,
                The image that her prey would wish to see!
                In Delphi, where I came by sea-ward route,
                Some soldiers of King Laius lay in wait,
                I thought it was but chance they found me there
                - For we were still at war -
                But now suspect the touch of her foul hand.

138

CHRYSIPPUS: Forget her now,
                Her list of crimes extends beyond belief.
                Acquaint me with the pain which dogs you so,
                That I may be a source of kind relief.

OEDIPUS: Oh Chrysippus, I know not what to say.
                How can a man make known his deepest fears?
                What Fate decrees must happen - That's the law!
                Regardless of the horror of those deeds!

CHRYSIPPUS: Be calm my friend.
                You've known my love, and know that in my heart,
                I hold you in like manner to myself.
                Your sorrows are my sorrows. Share your pain
                That we may, by division, break its hold,
                And bind our hearts against it in one whole.

                (They embrace again.)

OEDIPUS: Oh Chrysippus,
                Why ever did I turn my back on you?
                True Goodness never found so pure a home.

CHRYSIPPUS: Come,
                Cast off this cloak, I'll find you fresh attire.
                We'll take ourselves indoors where we may find,
                Good food, and soothing wine to quench your thirst,
                And then you can acquaint me with your worst.

                (Exit Oedipus with his arm around Chrysippus.)

                END OF ACT 3 SCENE 1

ACT 3 SCENE 2

The court of Laius

(Laius is reading a scroll. A storm is blowing outside. Enter proteus.)

PROTEUS: You sent for me, my lord?

LAIUS: Ah! Proteus. My trusty friend. What news?

PROTEUS: None my liege. The storm is wild,
              And looks to grow in anger through the night.
              But 'cept for this, our realm is still at peace.
              Although, some parts of Thebes report a plague,
              Which claims a life or two.

LAIUS: A plague?

PROTEUS: Aye. There are diverse reports.
              Some say a leper - who's vanished without trace -
              Came in and brought this ague in his wake.
              While others claim it is the time of year,
              When pestilence and famine both are ripe.
              No matter which, it will affect but few,
              And soon will run the measure of its course.

LAIUS: That is good news. These superstitious curs,
              Who scour our daily markets, looking mean,
              And waste their life with gossiping and lies,
              Soon turn the smallest matter on its head,
              And point it to the overthrow of kings!
              Tomorrow is the high point of our year,
              King Pelops and his court arrive at noon
              To sign these final papers for the peace,
              Which I've already printed with my seal.
              It would not do to have his visit linked,
              In any way, with this fresh rash of plague.

PROTEUS: I'll stem the news myself,
              And see those mouths stay mum,
              Which urge the market rabble on to heat.
              Although it is not easy in this clime,
              For some men find it harder to be good,

140

Now that our warring nations live at peace.
For many who, in wartime, seem at peace,
Merely vent their spleen through national rage.
But when the war is o'er,
Find they must control their own desires.

LAIUS: And is this so impossible to do?

PROTEUS: There's many out of work who will not try,
To rearrange their lives to suit their fate,
But stir up angry voices 'gainst the state,
And this way give expression to their hate!

LAIUS: I know this well enough. Tis every ruler's bane.
The rabble wants a life giv'n o'er to play,
But do not want to work to earn their pay.
How can I ever make this nation great,
When they fill up their minds with petty hates?
Have we not shown them ways to live their lives?
Pointed out directions; set them goals?
Does Chrysippus not model all that hope,
Exemplify what each man can become?

PROTEUS: Indeed he does,
A fine example for us all to take.
But though he is a model for our hope,
There's many wish that he was not so good.

LAIUS: What do you mean? You think his life's at risk?

PROTEUS: No. No. He's touched too many hearts.
They do not wish him harm.
Tis more, that he attains his grace with ease,
While others must work hard for that same praise.
To men of sense this seems completely just,
But unjust men would rather see the just,
Suffer more than those who are unjust.

LAIUS: But that's absurd!
It turns the whole of nature on its head.

PROTEUS: Tis merely what I hear the people say.

LAIUS: Then they are fools! Unworthy of my love,
And would be better dead than living here!
But hold!

I should not rail at you. You are a friend,
Who knows the common people are like sheep,
And blindly follow moods and current trends,
Without the slightest thought of what it means.
Why should they vex me so?
No. No. They are not worth my rage.
Let's to our business.
Tomorrow, as I said,
King Pelops and his court are due at noon.
We're ready to receive them in good kind,
And many entertainments are laid on,
To make a hearty welcome to our land.
And then again at night,
To further show our pleasure at this peace,
A banquet is prepared,
With dances, music, food, and ample wine.
But this is not your charge.
For I have set aside a special task,
Much closer to the purse-strings of my heart,
Than all this mindless revelry reveals.

PROTEUS: Tell on.
I'll do my best to serve you how I can.

LAIUS: Pelops' wife, Hippodamia,
You met her on that hill before the peace...

PROTEUS: I remember it well.
A dark and secret creature I recall,
And one I would not trust to call my friend.

LAIUS: That's her!
The very living essence of deceit!
At all times keep her hands within your eyes,
Lest she attempt some harm upon our court.

PROTEUS: You think she'll take your life?

LAIUS: No. No. Not mine. But Chrysippus.
So always keep your guard,
And follow her where'er she's want to go.
They stay but for the feast tomorrow night,
And then are gone.
She cannot do much harm in that short time,
And you shall guarantee that this proves true.

142

PROTEUS: I'll be her constant shadow through these hours,
             And if she shows the slightest trace of hate,
             My sword will make an end of all her woe.

LAIUS: Good man. I trust you, and your sword.
             But do not act too rashly o'er this point,
             Remember she's a queen and must have def'rence due.
             Now get abed, this storm grows with the night,
             Tis time our dreams put all our cares to flight.

             (*They both exit*)

                    END OF ACT 3 SCENE 2

ACT 3 SCENE 3

A corridor in the court of Thebes late at night. a storm is blowing without enter Chrysippus and Oedipus from one direction.

CHRYSIPPUS: Our happy conversation's kept us late,
I did not realise how high the moon,
Had climbed into the eye of this wild storm.

OEDIPUS: Time has no meaning when it's spent with you,
The hours have taken wing and fuelled our talk,
And shown us where eternity abides.

CHRYSIPPUS: And we have talked too long and must to bed.
Look, (*showing him a door.*)
Herein lies your chamber for the night,
Provided with soft tapers and good wine,
And all the needful requisites for sleep.

OEDIPUS: Oh Chrysippus,
Your kindness shames the very gods themselves.

CHRYSIPPUS: Sleep well,
I trust your night will prove a restful boon.
Tomorrow I shall make your presence known
To Laius and the household of his court,
Till then, adieu, and many pleasant dreams.

(They embrace.)

OEDIPUS: Sweet dreams to you,
And may tomorrow speed its passage here.

CHRYSIPPUS: Goodnight.

(Exit Chrysippus in the direction they came.)

OEDIPUS: Goodnight.

(Watching him go)

Sweet faithful child how happy am I now

144

To find myself within your love again.
How foolish was I when I spoke of war,
And ridiculed the vision you upheld,
For I have tasted hardship here in life
And see more clearly what it is you show,
And would be loathe to lose what I have found.

(*Enter Jocasta wearing her shawl and carrying a torch she comes from the other direction and does not see Oedipus at first as she hurries along the corridor. At last she sees him.*)

JOCASTA: Oh!
I had not thought this corridor in use.

OEDIPUS: Forgive me madam if I made you start.
I am a guest of Chrysippus this night.

JOCASTA: A friend of Chrysippus?
He made no mention of an extra guest.

OEDIPUS: He did not know that I'd arrived in Thebes,
I've only just acquainted him of this.
T'was most remiss,
But circumstances laid it out that way.

(*She observes him*)

JOCASTA: I know you, yet I know I know you not.
You seem somehow, familiar to my eyes,
And yet,
I swear I've never seen your face before.

OEDIPUS: Forgive me mam. (*He does a flourishing bow*)
My name is Oedipus,
I was a captain in King Pelops ranks,
Before this welcome peace, restored our lands.

JOCASTA: Ah. Oedipus. So you are Oedipus.
Your fame has travelled far across our land,
But you are dead, or so we thought,
For Chrysippus has often mourned your loss.

OEDIPUS: Then I have been reborn,
For if I'm dead, you converse with a ghost.

JOCASTA: You are no ghost of that fact I'm assured,

And yet,
You have an air that haunts me like a dream,
Some distant harking to a former time;
A memory, a trace of something lost,
Buried in the past like something dead.

OEDIPUS: There have been times when I have wished me dead,
             And walked eternal Hades as a ghost,
             But now rejoice in being so well alive,
             When creatures such as you inhabit earth.

JOCASTA: *(Embarrassed by this compliment)*
             Oh. You flatter me, yet know not who I am.

OEDIPUS: Your name will only grace your perfect form,
             Not alter it beyond the shape I see.
             A name confines in sounds the thing it names,
             And locks it in this charm that we may keep,
             The beauty of its form forever fresh,
             Recalling it at will, for pleasure's sake,
             When it has long departed from our sight.

JOCASTA: You are haughty child indeed,
             And work these words beyond their usual sense,
             And yet I feel no malice in your tongue.

OEDIPUS: Ye gods forbid
             If ever I should speak unwell of you!
             Madam,
             Your beauty is a treasure rarely seen,
             And wastes itself within this barren court.
             I feel, within my heart, a burning glow,
             And long to be acquainted with you more.

JOCASTA: You are too young to flatter me like this.

OEDIPUS: I am too old to waste a moment more,
             Parted from the pleasure of your sight.

JOCASTA: You jest.

OEDIPUS: Madam I do not!
             My heart is beating faster than the hooves,
             Of four and twenty chargers in a race,
             Where life or death are proffered as the stakes.
             I have not felt a power as strong as this,

Since first I knew the heady scents of love,
But even they seem stale to this sweet air,
Which hovers like a perfume round your form.

(He touches her on the cheek, gently.)

JOCASTA: Fie! Be gone! Do not touch me so!

(She turns away.)

[aside] Oh what a force of passion fills my loins.
My body burns. Desire is rampant here.
Oh how I long to move in his strong arms,
Surrender all my womanhood to him,
And satisfy those needs I most deny.
But cannot! for my marriage vows forbid!

OEDIPUS: Oh madam, do not fear the flames of love,
I feel them too,
Consuming every ounce of living flesh,
And filling me with Passion's heady brew.
Do not reign in what you would gladly give,
But let it flow for I desire it too.

(He touches her cheek)

JOCASTA: No-oh!
You are too forward with this ardent talk!
Tis only minutes since we first have met
But now you run us headlong into love.
Reign in your tongue before you cause offence.

OEDIPUS: Who makes the laws which govern how love runs?
I feel that I have known you all my life,
And but return to claim what is my own.
Is not first-sighted love the purest form?
I feel my blood rejoicing in this sight,
And coursing through my veins like living streams,
Pounding on these banks which hold it in.
I see you feel it too;
Those breathless gasps, the rapture in your eye,
That restless agitation of your feet.
Here,
Let me take you gently by the hand,
And soothe the ruthless pulse of violent love.

147

(He moves closer and takes hold of her hands.)

JOCASTA: No-oh!
            This is not proper for the role I play.

OEDIPUS: Do not deny the passion that you feel.
            Be kind, and let me kiss those vibrant lips,
            And press that heaving breast against my own.

JOCASTA: No-oh.

OEDIPUS: One kiss is all I ask.

JOCASTA: No...

(He kisses her lightly.)

Oh Oedipus, your kiss has set me free!

(She falls into his arms. They kiss passionately for a long time.)

Oh Oedipus,
For twenty years these feelings have been trapped,
Pent up in this cold body all that time,
But now you've set me free to live again,
Destroyed that stony mask of passive care,
Which I have worn to hide my true estate.
Now you have turned your sunny love on me,
And freed me to become what I should be,
The sensual, vibrant, woman that I am.
Oh how I feel this heat run through my veins,
And set alight my heart and all my cells,
As if it gave new birth to all my being.
Come, hold me close, and taste my lips again,
Fill me with richness of your love.

(They kiss again.)

OEDIPUS: My chamber door is here,
            Why do we not retire from this cold space,
            And find some warmer comfort in my bed.

JOCASTA: But Oedipus, you know not yet my name.

OEDIPUS: Tonight we'll count love's pleasure as our gains,
            Tomorrow will be soon enough for names.

(They exit into his chamber)

END OF ACT 3 SCENE 3

END OF ACT THREE

ACT 4 SCENE 1

The castle battlements of the court of Thebes.

(It is four am. The storm is at its height, thunder, lightning, driving rain. Chrysippus enters. He holds up his arms and addresses the sky)

CHRYSIPPUS: Abate storm!
Run your rain-wet tears back into clouds
And rush those clouds full-laden back to sea,
To blow tempestuous breaths on other shores.
Hear me! Hear me! Hear me!

(The storm abates)

This night my mind has filled with pure clear light
And shown me sights that few men live to see.
Come light,
Fill this hollow darkness with your glow,
Rekindle here the vibrance of my dream,
And bathed me in the brilliance of your show.

(The sky begins to fill with light)

Come. Come. Come.
Ye spirits of the depths, and of the heights,
And ye protectors too, who guard us all,
Shine down your light and show yourself to view.
Light. Light. Light. Vibrant shining light!
Send your radiant wisdom through the skies,
To kiss the inner sanctum of our eyes.
Come music too, lilt us from this world,
Raise up your heavenly voices to our praise,
And bathe us in your cool, melodic, rays.

(Sweet heavenly music begins)

Ah, such soothing sounds.
And you, ye fragrant perfumes of the earth,
Pomade your sweetest scents upon this air,
And fill our lungs with incense fit for gods.
Bathe me. Bathe me. Fill me with your love,

150

And re-create on earth your heaven above.
Ahh! (*He faints*)

(*Enter Lysias*)

LYSIAS: What heavenly sound is this?
            What music from on high delights my ears?
            And all this light, from some great form divine,
            Whence comes the blissful virtue of its rays?
            Am I awake,
            Or do I drift in slumbers endless coils,
            Enwrapt within the mists of hazy sleep,
            And dream this heavenly world presented here?

(*He notices Chrysippus*)

            What's this? 'Tis Chrysippus! Asleep?

(*He crosses to him and shakes him.*)

            Chrysippus! Chrysippus!
            What ails you? Are you ill? Wake up! Wake up!

CHRYSIPPUS: Ah. Lysias.
            My dear, sweet, lovely, gentle Lysias.
            To wake from sleep and see your kindly face,
            What softer, smooth transition could one wish?

LYSIAS: Your voice is strange. Your looks unkindly wild.
            What happened here?
            Why are you still abroad at this late hour?
            And why reclining here beneath the stars,
            Not settled, fast asleep, upon your bed?

CHRYSIPPUS: A dream. A precious, godly, dream.
            Far greater than your eyes have ever seen,
            Or all your conscious thought could ever scheme.

LYSIAS: Here, take my arm, sit down upon this wall
            And draw yourself together 'fore you speak.
            You are unwell,
            And need the soothing comfort of some balm.

(*He helps Chrysippus up, but Chrysippus shakes off his hand.*)

CHRYSIPPUS: Put off this fretful frown! I'm not unwell,

	But overcome with joy!
	T'was raw unbridle joy unhinged me here!
LYSIAS:	What joy? What words are these you speak?
CHRYSIPPUS:	Look in my eyes, imbibe the truth therein!
LYSIAS:	Your eyes are burning fires alive with light,
	And flash upon my face like noonday sun.
	What made them thus? What's happened to you here?
CHRYSIPPUS:	Oh Lysias,
	If only words could shape the things I've seen,
	Then I could make you tremble with delight,
	Leap firmaments, and vanish into space,
	See in one sweep the whole ascent of man,
	And realize at once how life began.
	But hark! (*he listens to the music.*)
	How crude our mundane voices come to sound,
	When heavenly notes resound within our ears.
LYSIAS:	Your mood indeed is strange. Are you unwell?
CHRYSIPPUS:	Oh Lysias,
	I leap the very confines of your thought,
	And cannot be constrained within such terms.
	'Well', 'unwell', these words are void of sense,
	And cannot circumscribe my present state!
LYSIAS:	Then say what does befall?
	For I am at a loss to know your mood.
CHRYSIPPUS:	This night I've had a dream,
	A dream more strange than any I have dreamt:
	A vision of what life should truly be,
	And what in time I know we shall become.
	I pulse full-pelt the richness of its shock
	But lack a sense of rhythm to convey,
	The smallest, finite, portion of its ray.
	Oh heavenly bliss that we should end this way!
LYSIAS:	Your voice and all your being,
	Speak volumes of some strange and altered state.
	I know not what to say,
	'Cept madmen seem your natural next of kin.

CHRYSIPPUS: It may be madness moves me as you say,
              But I would rather hold this maddened state,
              Than live your homely life which smacks of death.

LYSIAS: You're drunk!
              Transformed into some demon 'gainst your will!

CHRYSIPPUS: Then fill me with the nectar of this drink,
              Till I'm o'er-cloyed and leap this world for good!
              Sweet Lysias, I'm evolved!
              Transmuted and transformed beyond myself,
              Into some transcendental form of being!
              Feel you not these changes taking place?

LYSIAS: You now confirm what I did think before,
              That you have leapt the bounds of human sense,
              And course upon a world where madmen live.

CHRYSIPPUS: Then this is true! Mad! Merry-merry, mad!
              A lunatic below the sparkling moon.
              Come moon, I'll sing you out of sleep.

              (He sings - as he sings the moon begins to shine brightly)

              Your daughter's silver moonbeams
              Delight the earth below,
              Come shine your lunar light-beams
              And soothe our endless woe.

              Come rays of light from heaven
              Come gods, come goddess too,
              Come creatures from the nether world
              Raise up your comfort do.

              For we are but sweet angels
              Who share a life divine,
              Rejoice amid your splendour,
              For now and for all time.

              Oh, your daughter's silver moonbeams
              Delight the earth below,
              Come shine your lunar light-beams
              And soothe our endless woe.

              *(A huge wheel-like structure appears behind them. {The Tibetan
              Wheel of Life.} There are six areas or 'realms'. They are lit up*

153

by the soft milky-white light of the moon. The silent creatures
from each realm inhabit the areas and move as they are
described. they are:- gods: titans: humans: animals: hungry
ghosts and beings in hell.) [This could also be done as a
procession each of the realms proceeding across the stage as he
describes their silent passing. Different coloured light for each
realm.]

LYSIAS: What Magic show is this?

CHRYSIPPUS: Tis but the fading traces of my dream.
      View here, the yawning spectrum of all life!
      Come my beauties, come!
      These spectral worlds contain all sentient beings,
      Who're subject to the wheel of life and death,
      And float upon a sea of self-made woe.
      They rise from realm to realm by goodly deeds,
      Or fall from realm to realm by actions foul!
      There, at the top, resplendent in their pride,
      Reside the heavenly beings that we call gods;
      Who live in pleasure, satisfy all whims,
      And have no need to thus improve their lot.
      Next Titans - angry beings who seek for power -
      And jealously make war upon the gods,
      To vent their senseless fury and destroy,
      What they, through their own failings, can't enjoy.
      Below, the realm of Man, wherein we live,
      And have the best of all worlds here on earth,
      For we can, through our efforts, change and grow,
      And leap beyond the confines of this show.
      Then there, the sleepy realm of doleful beasts,
      Who dwell in fear and sloth and procreate,
      Quite unaware of any other state.
      Next, hungry ghosts, who endlessly desire,
      And crave and grasp at food which never can,
      Satisfy their underlying pain.
      Last, beings in hell, who burn in ceaseless fire,
      And suffer countless torments for the ill,
      Which they, in former times, did once inflict
      When they were wont to torture, maim, and kill.
      These beings now show themselves before your eyes,
      That you may see how life and death arise,
      And know the frail condition of our lives.
      Say now, who is the madman running wild?

(He dances about)

Oh Joy! Joy! Joy!
That we should be alive at such a time!

LYSIAS: But Chrysippus come back!
              Explain this sight to me.
              Am I awake and living, breathing, air,
              Or do I simply dream this vision here?

CHRYSIPPUS: You dream it! For they are but phantom shapes,
              And like this tinsel world soon fade away.

              (*He claps his hands. the dumb show ceases.*)

              This world we see is like some vast, long, dream,
              Made concrete by the workings of our mind.
              It has no more solidity than thought,
              Which comes unbidden, vanishes to naught,
              And leaves no trace or trail that we may plot.
              Tonight I saw it all. T'was all revealed.
              For me this whole charade has been exposed.
              I have no fear of death, for I can't die.
              No more than I can live upon this earth.
              For we are but mere fragments of a dream,
              Mere nothingness! The lie to what we seem!
              The shadow flitting substances supreme!
              A void of voidness! Orphans of no-scheme!
              Do you share now the madness of my dream?

              (*He runs about madly again*)

LYSIAS: Be still! Be still! Unfold yourself to me,
              For either, you are raving out of sense,
              Or else you've seen some vision of the Truth.
              Divulge which one is true?

CHRYSIPPUS: The former and the latter, both are true!

LYSIAS: But say, before you dance away again,
              What was this magic power induced those shapes,
              Which you brought here before our very eyes?

CHRYSIPPUS: There was no power!
              T'was but your selfless love and faith in me,
              Suspended for a while your Reasons's hold,
              And let you taste the essence of my dream.

155

But patience! Wait! I rush too far ahead,
O'ertake myself before I have begun.
Here, sit you down, I'll tell you of my night,
And fill your mind with sights you ne'er have seen.

LYSIAS: But...

CHRYSIPPUS: Be calm! I'll tell you line by line.
This storm, which raged and raved above our heads,
First woke me from a sweat-infested sleep,
Where Darkness loomed above me like cold Death,
Choking all the hope within my breast,
And causing me to think that I was dead.
For I could see upheavals in this world,
Made manifest in this ungainly storm,
And flashed across the sky for all to read.
For deep within our labyrinthine earth
Two forces fought to give their essence birth:
The first, dark brooding Blackness and his horde,
Determined to envelope us in night;
The second, shining Goodness, with Her light,
Intent to show Mankind his true delight,
And midwife in this world Her infant bright!
Across this sky, their violent struggle ranged,
Until Dark-Blackness mustered all his fiends,
And seemed about to crush this babe for good.
But no! Its birth was our release!
For suddenly, I fainted from all sense,
And leapt into the air unformed and free,
And was no more confined by this crude flesh.
For I'd become some golden, godlike, being,
Who viewed the vast deep emptiness of space,
And shone his gentle light o'er all Mankind.
For Mankind is adrift on some cruel sea
- An ocean full of pain and endless woe -
Which stretches out beyond our finite time,
And fills the whole enormity of space.
And as I cast my gaze across this sea,
I saw all life arise and then decay,
Impermanence, the lord and god of all,
And Change, the constant master of this squall.
And as I viewed this folly with new eyes,
Tears of white compassion wet my cheeks,
And fell onto those suff'ring beings below.
Then they looked up, transformed by what they'd felt,
For Kindness and Compassion rule this world,

More surely than the pain wherein they dwelt.
And as I stooped to draw them from that sea,
A million, million, lights lit up the sky,
And filled the vast dark black of endless space.
For they'd expanded, opened up their hearts,
Revealed their treasured essence pure and bright,
And drowned that world of hell in golden light.
Then they arose on vibrant, rainbow, trails,
With love and laughter sparkling through their eyes,
And blazed their selfless beauty 'cross the skies.
And as they spiralled high above that sea,
I saw at once that they had all become,
Pure Perfect Beings! Enlightened! Deathless! Free!
Then I awoke, still coursing with this joy,
Came out to view this sky, and taste this air,
Rejoicing that I'd seen what life can be,
And knowing that we are, forever, free!
Oh Lysias,
Does this not take the breath from out your lungs,
And vindicate your wildest, maddest, dreams?
That we should be such brilliant, glowing, beings!
Rejoice! Rejoice! Mankind can e're rejoice!
And tremble at the splendour of his being!

LYSIAS: My dear, impassioned, friend,
This is a mighty vision you have seen,
And holds much hidden truth within its form.
And you have changed beyond your normal self,
So that, I do not now, know who you are.

CHRYSIPPUS: I know not yet myself,
But feel what e'er I am, is good and true,
And vindicates all that I've ever learned,
About our single purpose on this earth.

LYSIAS: But what will you do now?

CHRYSIPPUS: I'll seek to make my vision known to all,
For we can, through our efforts, make ourselves;
Create compassion; free ourselves from hate;
And rise above the workings of our fate.
For, with the help of Laius, I can cause,
Throughout all Thebes, the passing of new laws,
More keeping with the spirit of my dream,
Until such time as all Men live and be
What they, in their true essence, really are.

(Distant thunder rolls. The sky darkens.)

But come,
We'll talk at length again, about these sights,
And how 'tis best to make their contents known.
But not tonight, for look:
The storm has drawn its heavy mantle round,
And chased my brilliant vision from the sky,
Heralding dull morning in its wake.
Today my father comes to view this court
And I must stand attendance on his needs.
We shall in time explore these thoughts in full,
And find a way to share this precious jewel.

(Thunder and lightning)

But let's go in. This storm is not yet still.

(They exit with their arms around each other)

END OF ACT 4 SCENE 1

ACT 4 SCENE 2

Oedipus' chambers. 7am. the following morning. Jocasta is seated brushing her hair, a well used bed in the background, Oedipus pacing up and down.

OEDIPUS: The queen of Thebes! The royal wife of Thebes!
                      How could it be much worse?

JOCASTA: You said last night,
                      That names could safely wait until the dawn.

OEDIPUS: Jocasta, queen of Thebes,
                      What name is that to hide from any man,
                      Especially as I am your husband's guest?

JOCASTA: Be not afeared, he'll never need to know,
                      He does not care a whit for what I do.

OEDIPUS: But what of me? How do I behave,
                      Knowing that I trespassed with his wife?

JOCASTA: I'd smile if I was you, a secret inward smile,
                      To show the world contempt for all its rules.

OEDIPUS: You sphinx,
                      Riddling with me here in Time's cruel sands,
                      As if this was some jest to please the court.

(She proffers her hand back to him; he is standing behind her)

JOCASTA: Oh do not be so sore, my little child,
                      For was it not a rich and warm affair,
                      A night that you would sue to live again?
                      Here, kiss my hand, and tell me I speak true.

(He comes forward and takes her hand then kisses her cheek)

OEDIPUS: To taste again the pleasures of last night,
                      I'd fight a thousand battles, kill more foes,
                      Than all who fell in this ten years of war.

JOCASTA: Then stay with me and give your love again.

(H*e breaks away*)

OEDIPUS: No!
             For you are still his wife, and this is wrong!

JOCASTA: You are a child. A spoiled and whining child.
             You think I owe allegiance to this man,
             Who held me thrall to Negligence and Pain
             Mapped out a life of frigid self-denial,
             So I might play the role of faithful wife.
             You've set me free, released me from these chains,
             You think I'll let him tie those knots again?
             These twenty years I've plotted for his death,
             But have not had an ally in these plans.
             Now you and I together can contrive
             To end his reign and oust him from his throne.

OEDIPUS: Be silent fiend! This is not fitting talk!
             I do not wish him dead, he is mine host,
             And I the guilty party in his house.

JOCASTA: Where stands my brave and valiant soldier now?
             Look what you've become!
             A little boy, afraid of some old man,
             Who'd crumble at the roaring of your voice.

OEDIPUS: Your cruelty transfixes me with fear.
             Do women have a premium on such thought,
             Or is it merely royalty alone?

JOCASTA: When men are weak, then women must be strong.

OEDIPUS: Huh. Then you'll find Hippodamia of your sort,
             A sister in these devious trains of thought.
             You should merge well, and find each other fun,
             You have so much in common, so it seems.

JOCASTA: Hippodamia, you knew her too?

OEDIPUS: I knew her wicked mind.

JOCASTA: Oh Oedipus,
             Be not unkind, this rage I feel is just.
             These twenty years I've been a frigid wreck,
             A wraith that's hunted endlessly for love.

160

I have a right to vent my fury now!
But calm your fears, for these are only words,
I do not wish him dead, but merely gripe,
That he has held me prisoner for so long.
Although, if he should die,
It would allow our passion greater scope,
To probe the furthest reaches of our love.
We could have children, offspring of my womb,
And live like man and wife as we two should.
But come, hold me in your arms,
Your sultry ways are unbecoming here.
We can, if we are careful, still maintain,
Our secret love, and none will ever know.

(*He moves to her they embrace.*)

OEDIPUS: You women are the same,
              Devious and warped beyond all hope.

JOCASTA: And men like you have one thing on their mind.

(*They kiss*)

BLACKOUT!

END OF ACT 4 SCENE 2

161

ACT 4 SCENE 3

The following morning in the main chamber of Thebes, Proteus is ordering soldiers about.

PROTEUS: You men array yourself around the room,
            And mingle best you can within the crowd,
            We do not wish too crude a show of force.
            Your others take the chambers to the east,
            And allocate a man to every room,
            But have him well concealed from common view....

            (*Enter Laius.*)

LAIUS: Proteus!

PROTEUS: Aye, my liege.

LAIUS: A word.

PROTEUS: [*To Laius*] At once.
            [T*o Men*] Get you hence, assemble at your posts,
            And see you are alert and set by noon.
            I'll bring you more instruction in due time.

            (*The soldiers dismiss, Proteus crosses to Laius.*)

            I've stationed men throughout the palace grounds,
            And many more will mingle with the court,
            Lest there should be a need for force of arms...

LAIUS: How did you sleep?

PROTEUS: Sleep?
            Why, well, I think? I had not giv'n it thought.

LAIUS: You woke not with the storm?

PROTEUS: The storm was loud, and woke me several times,
            But yet I did sleep well.

LAIUS: [*aside*] Then this confirms the storm was sent for me.

PROTEUS: My liege, you look distraught, is there some fault,

Some service I have failed?

LAIUS: No. No.
                Your service has been faultless through the years.
                Or so I've always thought...

PROTEUS: And yet still is!
                My duty is to serve you best I can,
                And I have always striven to that end.
                If there has been some lapse, or thoughtless fault,
                Acquaint me with it now,
                That I may set my record straight at once.

LAIUS: Some years ago, some score of years ago,
                When you were but a servant in this court,
                I called upon your help in one small deed,
                Which you, with faithful vigour, undertook.

PROTEUS: Some deed?

LAIUS: Yes. A child.
                A babe I wanted banished from our land,
                For reasons that you did not need to know.
                I ordered you to take this child away,
                And kill it some far distance from our court,
                That we would not be tarnished with its death.

PROTEUS: Aye, and that I did,
                Obeying every letter of your word.

LAIUS: You killed this child? There was no soft reprieve?

PROTEUS: None. Or none that I supplied.
                That child has long since ceased to take in breath,
                Or rend the air with its incessant cries.

LAIUS: You're sure?

PROTEUS: Sure?
                I rammed a sapling twig between its heels,
                And left the bleeding urchin there to die,
                Upended and alone on Cithaeron's hill.
                What child could e'er escape a fate like that?

LAIUS: None. None.
                [aside] Save one that was in cohorts with the gods.

163

[*aloud*] Then you are certain that this child is dead?

PROTEUS: My liege, if I may overstep my place and rank,
             This child expired some twenty years ago,
             Why do you now raise doubts that it is dead?
             Has some event cast doubts upon my skill?

LAIUS: Events are breaking o'er us all the time,
             That make us doubt the truth of what we feel.

PROTEUS: I do not comprehend?

LAIUS: Last night, while I lay restless on my bed,
             I had a dream, a vision of this child,
             And saw him limping cruelly down that hill,
             His face, all hate and anger, swoll'n with fire,
             And I, the teeth-clenched victim, of his ire.
             And as he came these words went through my head:
             "This child will seek revenge. This child will seek revenge."
             On and on they pounded through my brain,
             Like some unreal cantation for the dead,
             Until I could not think of aught but them.
             The howling wind took up this haunting chant,
             And crashed against the shutters of my room,
             Until his marching footsteps could be heard,
             Limping through the corridors of time,
             And pounding out his vengeance on my head.
             And then, before my face, I saw his eyes,
             Enlarged and swoll'n with blood, like one insane.
             He'd crept into the palace, stolen my wife,
             And trapping me within my bedding sheets,
             Began to carve me up like suckling pig.
             And as I bled, he snatched my sacred ring,
             Took up my robe and donned my regal crown,
             Proclaimed himself the rightful king of Thebes,
             And ended me upon those blood-stained sheets.

PROTEUS: Tis but a dream, my liege, a nightmare you've endured.
             This storm has swept your mind along its course
             And filled your ears with anger from its noise,
             Raising fitful visions in your dreams.
             They have no link with life, or what is real.

LAIUS: But what is real, and wherein does it lie?
             Our eyes inform our mind of what they see,
             And when we see the world, we call it real,

164

But these dark visions shone before my eyes
More real and true than any waking sight.
You seem to me mere shadow in this light
While he shone out a living, breathing, form!

PROTEUS: It was a dream! A nightmare and a dream.
This child is dead, and cannot do you harm,
Be not afraid of nightmares, or of dreams.

LAIUS: No!
This was no simple dream; those images were real!
This is some premonition of foul deeds,
A prophecy of darkness and decay.
This child will take my life!

PROTEUS: The child is dead! I killed him on that hill.
There was no hope in hell that he'd survive.
This storm has merely touched some spark of guilt,
That you have lately harboured for this deed.

LAIUS: Ahh. That could be so.
My mind has had occasion these past months
To dwell upon the fitness of that act.
But you are certain that the child is dead?

(Proteus withdraws his sword.)

PROTEUS: As dead as is the metal in this sword.

(He drops it to the ground.)

See, it falls,
A useless, weighty, object, to the ground,
Cold, and stiff, and lifeless like the dead -
As is this child!

LAIUS: Your words are good, 'tis what I longed to hear.
This stormy night, these plans for this day's feast,
And Hippodamia's presence in our court,
Have played upon the weakness of my brain,
And caused my restless night and fitful dreams.
I'm better now. I knew you'd done the deed,
But Doubt arose, and I in fright succumbed,
And helped it build a temple in my brain,
Where all my insecurity could dwell,
And multiply itself 'till I was ill.

Tis strange how fear abides,
And simple doubt can tease us out of sense.
But get you in,
And not a word of this to any ear.
I'll come inspect your soldiers in good time.

PROTEUS: Thank you, my liege.
No word of this shall ever cross my lips.
Adieu.

(E*xit Proteus*)

LAIUS: Adieu.
Oh how I longed to hear what you have said.
Imagination fires our feelings up
Until we can no longer sense what's true,
Or make a sharp distinction 'tween our dreams
And what we come, in life, to call 'the real'.
But I still fear these actions from the past,
They overhang my thinking like some cloud,
And spring before my mind like lighted shapes,
That frame in perfect detail every deed,
Till I have time to see what I have done,
Inspect the actions, notice every flaw,
E'en taste the tastes, and smell the smells of time,
Enact and re-enact them o'er and o'er,
Until I seem to live in past events,
More fully than I do this present now.
Oh would that my past actions would dissolve,
And vanish like damp vapours in the air,
Not gather like a storm above my head,
To plague me with some retributive scene.
This night my stomach's been a pit of fear,
A fear I have not know for countless years,
Since first I tasted battle on the field.
But then it was a fear that I might die,
Might lose my life to some unsightly blow,
But now this fear, although it smacks of death,
Feels stronger in its massiveness and doubt.
And multiplies its horror to my mind.
Some great machine, some cosmic force unfolds,
Some token of my destiny reveals,
That I must suffer for my actions past,
And die the death of fools.

(*A trumpet sounds.*)

166

Hah! Their party is in sight.
My kingly tasks now call me back from hell.
How timely does the mundane interfere,
To shake this dark improvidence, I fear.

(E*xit Laius*)

END OF ACT 4 SCENE 3

ACT 4 SCENE 4

Hippodamia's chambers in the court of Thebes.

> (*Thyestes and Atreus run on boisterously. They are having a mock sword fight.*)

THYESTES: Have at you varlet! Prove yourself a man.

ATREUS: Begone cruel wretch, or taste this tempered steel,
For you are more a varlet than am I.

THYESTES: Then fight you fiend. I'll show who here is true.
Your running woman's legs defy your tongue.

> (*They fight. Thyestes strikes Atreus.*)

Ha! A wound! A strike! A perfect point to me.

ATREUS: Nay. Your eyes deceive your brain.

THYESTES: Then parry this.

> (*He strikes him again*)

ATREUS: Ahh!
Revenge! I'll have my sweet revenge.

> (*He knocks over a chair*)

Turn over, cur!

> (*Atreus trips Thyestes who falls over*)

THYESTES: Begone cruel king, you taste the taste of blood,
And swoop upon your foe, like carrion crows.
Would you devour a man while he is down?

ATREUS: When you are dead, they'll lay you in the ground,
So why not die now that you are lain down?

THYESTES: Begone! Begone! I live to fight again.

(He rises and they fight on)

ATREUS: Parry.

THYESTES: Fight you cowardly fiend.

               (Enter Pelops.)

PELOPS: Boys! Boys! Enough of all this noise,
               This court is not your own.
               Be mindful of the duties of a guest.
               Go! Take yourself indoors.
               Your mother's on her way,
               And needs her rest before this evening's feast.
               Go! Go! Obey me or you'll feel my wrathful hand!

               (The boys go off, sulkily. He rights the fallen chair.)

               Oh why did she invite these spoilsome brats?
               They run amok like jackals after prey,
               And do not heed a single word I say.
               How could a woman so refined as she,
               Give birth to such unruly brats as these?

               (Enter Hippodamia and Livia)

               Ah. My love, how are you now?

HIPPODAMIA: The better for the end of that cruel ride.
               My senses have been bumped quite out of sense.
               But you look tired and wracked with many ills.
               What grieves you so?

PELOPS: Your boys exhaust me. I wish they had not come.

HIPPODAMIA: I want them here they are my only sons.
               Tis but your lengthy years that make you tired.
               My boys are no more troublesome than most,
               Tis but a fault in you,
               Being so far distant from your early youth,
               You do forget how wild you were yourself.
               Sit down awhile and rest your weary head.

LIVIA: I'll fetch your luggage mam.

               (Exit Livia.)

169

PELOPS: *(He sits)* I'm glad to take this pressure off my feet,
Since early dawn I've paced my bedroom floor,
Praying that your illness would expire,
And set you free to journey here with me.
This endless month of torment has been foul,
And drained all sense of pleasure from my brain.
Tis good to see you looking well again.

HIPPODAMIA: Yes, yes.
I'm better now so do not fret you more.

(she looks round the room)

So this is how King Laius sees a queen,
A simple chamber draped in regal red,
But lacking more than necessary grace?

PELOPS: Tis functional my dear,
We're only here for one brief festal night.
And do not need more comfort than a bed.

HIPPODAMIA: I think I would have shown more wealth than this,
To any royal court which graced my shores.

PELOPS: It will suffice our needs.

HIPPODAMIA: My love,
Why do you not retire unto your room.
I shall unpack and rest myself awhile,
And make myself more ready for the court.
And you should do the same.

PELOPS: I do not have the energy to move.
I'd rather sit right here and drift away,
Be borne upon the comfort of sleep's wings,
And revel in the thought that you are near.

HIPPODAMIA: But I am near. Your room is next to mine.

PELOPS: *(e rises)* It seems a world away to my tired feet.

HIPPODAMIA: Tis but a thought, a trifle in our minds.
We never are apart while we have thought.
Now I must rest,
The arduours of this journey take their toll.

PELOPS: *(He kisses her.)* Rest well my love,
                     Tis good to see you back among the quick,
                     I had such fears that you might pass away,
                     Before that wretched fever left your frame.

HIPPODAMIA: Put up these fears, I am alive and well.
                     But go now, 'fore you set me on to weep,
                     For think you not I feared to lose you too?

PELOPS: Oh dearest love, you're tenderness itself.

                     (He *kisses her forehead.*)

HIPPODAMIA: Begone!
                     I'll melt into a schoolgirl once again,
                     If you maintain this flattery much more.

PELOPS: Farewell.

HIPPODAMIA: Farewell.

                     (He blows her a kiss and goes)

                     Oh what a tiresome fool you have become,
                     To dote upon my every word of praise!
                     I feel as if I bear you on my back,
                     And when I walk must carry you as well.
                     Have you not feet to stand on as your own?
                     But let that be.
                     If this night goes according to my plan,
                     I'll end you here along with all my foes.

                     (Thyestes and Atreus come running in.)

ATREUS: Mama. Mama.

HIPPODAMIA: What's wrong my dears?

THYESTES: Pelops raised his hands to strike us down.

ATREUS: Oh mama.
                     He was about to beat us with his cane.

THYESTES: Mama. Mama.

171

HIPPODAMIA: Be silent chicks,
That foul old man is weary of this life,
And seeks some softer realm to lay his head,
Which he 'forelong shall find is waiting here.
Pay no heed to his quirky, griping, ways,
But come to me instead.

(She draws them to her)

This night, sweet chicks, your fortune will be won,
And we shall see the end of all my work.
I'll call upon your help in some small deed,
Which you, through love for me, will gladly do.
Is this not so?

ATREUS: What deed is this mama?

HIPPODAMIA: I'll tell you in good time,
But do not fail to help me when I call.
You love your mama, don't you?

(Silence. The boys look at each other and then at their feet.)

Don't you boys?

(she hugs them to her)

Of course you do. The cat has got your tongue,
And makes you shy to speak your love to me.

(Enter Livia with a bag and a small box.)

But hush for now and take yourselves within.
I'm weary from the harshness of this ride,
And need some hours of rest to still my brain.
Go play, until I call for you again.

(They exit. Livia is placing the box on the side.)

Ahh Livia. What box is that?

LIVIA: Tis all those special potions you have made,
And detailed I should bring upon this voyage.

HIPPODAMIA: Good. I'll check them by and by.
The phial is there as well?

172

LIVIA: Everything your majesty desired.

HIPPODAMIA: Good. I'll send for you anon.

(*Livia curtsies and exits*)

(*she wrings her hands*)

Now draws on the climax of my plan,
And brings to ripe fruition all my schemes.
This night shall see my dream come to its end,
And sanction all the hopes I entertain:
My sons shall rule the whole estate of Greece,
And I will be the queen of all mankind.

(*She opens the box and takes out the phial*)

This phial contains some potion I have brewed,
To speed King Laius swiftly to his grave.
One drop placed on his lips while he's asleep,
And drawn into his body with the air,
Will end him 'fore that breath vacates his lungs.
This too, will snuff that stupid, doting, fool,
Who coos with love and reckons me his spouse.
I'll lace his night-time drink with its effects,
And he will kiss the world his last farewell.
My sons, I shall instruct, with knife and sword,
To take the life of Chrysippus, who sleeps,
With love, in all the bosoms of this court.
But I'll soon winkle love from their dull hearts
And point the blame for all those other deaths,
So squarely in the grip of his dead hands,
That none will dare to countermand his guilt.
Then I shall gather lilacs for the dead,
And show a face full-sorrowful and sore,
That pity will be heaped upon my frame,
Until there is no pity left to bear.
Ohh!
But what is this? What shadow circles here?
What is this evil darkness drapes my mind,
Like stormy clouds that rush to some far squall?

(*she swoons*)

Oh! I faint.

This seat will give me comfort for a while.

(*she sits*)

Tis but the heady wastage of our ride,
My senses have been shaken out of sorts,
And need some time to make me whole again.
Come breath, revive me with your charms,
And ease this panting, pressure I endure.
My heart beats like a dancer's furious drum,
That fashions out the steps that she must tread,
And forces her to dance beyond her ken.
Oh Heart,
Do not race so! I have much need of rest!
I sense some strange upheaval in myself,
And cannot fathom what I shall become,
But do not like the vision that I see.
What drives me on at this relentless pace,
Fulfilling these dark needs that I know not?
Some days I seem enwrapt in Fate's black shroud,
Which crushes all the feeling from my form,
And forces me to some unspoken end:
As if some pregnant moment had arrived,
And gave its birth to some new form of being;
Consumed by fury, driven by despair,
And sired by poisoned passions from my heart.
Oh heart, you race beyond all hope.
I must desist! And end these wretched plans.
Put paid to all this fever in my mind.
But no!
This weakness should not hold my spirits down.
Why should I not exalt the goals I've made?
My sons are worthy any here in court,
And I the finest woman living still,
Why should I not strive on?
Ooh! (*she holds her stomach*)
My pain returns again.
The voidness of my womb has made me ill,
And leaves me but a battered, empty, shell.
There then!
Is that not cause enough to carry on?
To seek revenge for all that awful deed,
And punish wretched Laius for his acts?
Yes! That is just cause indeed!
Draw in your fears and banish feckless doubt.
Direct your thinking to that needful end,

174

And do not waver from your chosen course,
Until your heart has had its full revenge!
Come night, draw on your darkest steeds,
And blind all eyes to my intended deeds.

END OF ACT 4 SCENE 4

END OF ACT FOUR

ACT 5 SCENE 1

(The Throne Room in the palace at Thebes

There are two raised thrones side by side at the back of the room, and a table laid with drinks and food downstage right.

A sennet and drums then Laius and Pelops enter in full regalia leading a train of both courts: Hippodamia, Arrian, Atreus, Livia, Watchman, Thyestes, Chrysippus, Lysias, Pelops, Lambrus, Pitheus, Jocasta, Oedipus, Cretheus, & Proteus. all {except Laius, Pelops, Cretheus and Proteus} wear masks. Laius and Pelops stop in front of the thrones, the others spread out around them. Proteus and Cretheus stand guard by Laius.

LAIUS: Come.
      This day of signing treaties is now through,
      And we, by this accord are thus made one,

      (he takes Pelops' hand and raises it in the air)

      And shall for many years both reign in peace.

      (applause)

      Well feasted we, and ready for more joy,
      And so our formal talk will henceforth cease.
      We shall with lighter thought now bless the night,
      And raise our spirits in this festal cheer.
      Your masks and robes disguise your persons well,
      So do not break the spell till we are through.
      Take up your partners, let this dance commence,
      And bless our peace with your light-footed tread.
      Our sovereignties will grace the show from here.

      (They sit, and music begins. the others choose a, supposedly, unknown partner:- Hippodamia with Chrysippus: Jocasta with Oedipus: Thyestes with Livia: Atreus with Arrian: Lambrus with Pitheus.)

THYESTES: Brother Atreus, you know which one is which?

ATREUS: Arrian is robed in emerald, green,
               While Livia is decked out in the red.

THYESTES: Let's to them quick before we miss our match.

OEDIPUS: Does my lady's heart still ache for love?

JOCASTA: Oedipus! Tis you. How knew you of my place?

OEDIPUS: The ring upon your finger shows your rank.

JOCASTA: Oh fie! The one thing I forgot. But no.
               Why curse it so?
               Tis fitting I should dance this dance with you,
               We'll celebrate our nuptials in its step.

LAMBRUS: Well, buxom wench, you look good meat to me.

               (*He pinches Pitheus's bottom*)

PITHEUS: I'll good meat you! You saucy cad! (*Strikes Lambrus*)

LAMBRUS: Ow! A spritely miss, I'll vouch.
               This dance will prove most flavoursome I see.

               (*he pats Pitheus's bottom*)

PITHEUS: Unhand me fiend! This flesh is mine.
               Not rump prepared for all, like butcher's meat.

LAMBRUS: Tis fleshy rump, that needs a seasoned touch,
               I'll tenderised it gently with these hands.

               (*he pinches Pitheus's bottom again*)

PITHEUS: Begone! I will not warn you more!

               (*Suddenly a chord is struck, they all bow and then begin a very
               formal masked dance. Conversation during the dance*)

HIPPODAMIA: You trip it well.

CHRYSIPPUS: Thank you, mam. You too, are light of foot,
               And glide like one well suited to this art.

ATREUS: Don't dance so fast,
               You'll need some forward motion for tonight.

177

ARRIAN: I'd dance all night and still have strength for you.

ATREUS: Fie! You know not who you mock!

ARRIAN: I know you well enough, you cheating rogue.

JOCASTA: Ha!
           The irony of this delightful dance,
           Fills me with a rich triumphant thrill.
           To think we can so brazenly make love,
           And none will know just what these masks conceal.

OEDIPUS: My lady has a cruel and wicked streak,
           Hell bent on wreaking vengeance on her king.

JOCASTA: Not vengeance, merely justice, pure and true.

LAIUS: Who is that man who dances with my wife?

PROTEUS: Tis Oedipus, Chrysippus's friend.

LAIUS: He draws too near by far.
           [*aside*] His actions echo those from that dark dream:
           "A man who steals my wife".
           I must beware lest he usurp my crown.
           But fie! What foolishness is this,
           To grace this act with overtures of fear,
           When tis but nothing more than wanton sport.

           (The dance finishes, applause.)

           Bravo! Bravo! Such finely measured steps.
           You all have proved the blessing to our day.
           Remove your masks, converse, and make new friends,
           And let this peace live lively in our court.

ATREUS: I'll celebrate this lively piece right here.
           (He grabs Arrian)

ARRIAN: Unhand me beast.

THYESTES: Aye, and I this one. *(He grabs Livia)*

LIVIA: Desists you foolish boy, you're not at home.
           Your mother is a figurehead of state,

178

And you a regal prince, so act your age!
These puerile acts will soil your royal name.

THYESTES: Tis you who soil my name,
By acting like some upstart, haughty, whore!

(*The other partners take off their masks.*)

LAMBRUS:& PITHEUS:TOGETHER: YOU!

PITHEUS: How dare you pinch my bum!

LAMBRUS: I did not know 'twas yours.

PITHEUS: Away with you. I am no cheapskate tart,
Who sells her flesh to every man in town.
I'll teach you not to tenderise my rump!

(*Pitheus chases Lambrus off, the others laugh.*)

HIPPODAMIA: Well, well, tis Chrysippus, my son.
We were indeed well matched.

CHRYSIPPUS: I did not know your ladyship could dance.

HIPPODAMIA: Nor I you.
Yet are there not but many things in life,
We know so little of?

CHRYSIPPUS: Indeed there are,
And many that I wish we all knew more.
But is your highness well?
I heard you had been troubled with a plague,
And were confined most sorely to your bed?

HIPPODAMIA: A trifling childish thing. A cold, no more than that,
T'was nothing of concern and soon thrown off.
I am in no way lacking in good health.

CHRYSIPPUS: Your majesty mistakes.
I meant no form of insult to your health,
But merely asked that I may wish you well,
Or offer some soft comfort for your pain.

HIPPODAMIA: I have no need of comforting from you!

PELOPS: (*to Hippodamia*) Join us my dear.
                   (*to Laius*) My queen is such a credit to our court,
                   I could not fill my role without her aid.

LAIUS: She dances well and chose a perfect mate.

                   (H*ippodamia approaches*)

PELOPS: Bravo my dear,
                   You glided like a swan upon the sea.

HIPPODAMIA: My lord is far too gracious with his tongue.

PELOPS: No. No. I flatter not a whit.
                   T'was nice to see you dancing with our son.

HIPPODAMIA: These masks obscured our partners from our choice.

PELOPS: (*to Hippodemia*) Tis good to see our Chrysippus so well.
                   (to Laius) He seems more manly since his sojourn here,
                   More self assured, matured, and full of joy,
                   And physically improved in every way.
                   You've done us proud.

LAIUS: I think he has matured, (*to Hippodemia*) as we have wisened
too.
                   (*to Pelops*) Your son has brought much credit to my court,
                   His thoughts and charming ways,
                   Have made a living heaven of my realm.
                   I cannot think why any wish him harm.

PELOPS: Wish him harm? What do you mean?
                   Who here could wish him harm?

HIPPODAMIA: I think King Laius jests,
                   There's no one here could wish to harm your son.

LAIUS: (*he smiles broadly at Hippodamia*)
                   A jest. A jest. Of course it was a jest.
                   I meant it as a metaphor for life.
                   Our court is full of people living still,
                   Who otherwise might easily be dead.
                   Oedipus, Chrysippus, Jocasta and myself:
                   Who knows,
                   Had not this state of welcome peace prevailed?

PELOPS: Ahh. The peace. The peace. I see now what you mean.
                 I did not take your metaphor aright,
                 But thought you meant some danger to my son.

HIPPODAMIA: King Laius has a sharp and witty tongue.

LAIUS: Indeed I have.
                 Diplomacy is such a needful skill,
                 Especially in affairs that touch the heart.
                 But come, (*he snaps his fingers*) I bring our spirits down,
                 Such talk is not conducive to our feast.

                 (*A servant approaches with goblets of wine.*)

                 This wine will fill our minds with festal thoughts,
                 And flush our cheeks the colour of its grape,
                 That we, in joyous pleasure, may partake.

CHRYSIPPUS: She snubbed me once again.

LYSIAS: Then let her be.
                 Why waste your breath on making peace with her,
                 When she would wage a war of hate 'gainst thee?

CHRYSIPPUS: No! Tis not a waste, but more a kind of test.
                 Tis easy to be friendly with one's friends,
                 Or freely give one's love to those one loves.
                 But shows far greater mastery of self,
                 If one can feel a selfless love for all,
                 Regardless of their kindness or their hate.
                 This, is what my vision would exalt,
                 And this, I'll do!

LYSIAS: Oh Chrysippus,
                 Your goodness is beyond all human thought.

CHRYSIPPUS: Tis not! and should not be so framed!
                 We all can love our enemies as friends,
                 And if we would attain that perfect state,
                 Not only can but must!

LYSIAS: Tis true,
                 You vision has no compromising traits,
                 But t'will take time to change the ways of men,
                 For they prefer being animals to saints.

181

THYESTES: A little wine to loosen up your legs.

LIVIA: Cur! (*she slaps him*)
              You are no better than a common beast,
              Who thinks of food and sex and nothing more.

THYESTES: Moo! That's sounds like fun,
              I'll play the bull, and you can play the cow.

              (*she grabs him roughly by the throat*)

LIVIA: Desist! I've warned you of this once.
              Stop now before you shame your mother here,
              And make a laughing stock of all our court,
              Or you will never take in breath again.

THYESTES: Ahh! Let go! You're choking me, you bitch!

LIVIA: Then learn to rule your lusts.

              (*she sets him free*)

THYESTES: (*coughing*) I'll settle you for this, you common whore!

LAIUS: Cretheus,
              Go tell my wife to mingle with the crowd,
              She showers too much attention on this man.

CRETHEUS: I shall my liege.

              (*Cretheus approaches Jocasta and bows*)

CRETHEUS: Madame,
              King Laius bids you circulate the crowd,
              Lest such prolonged attention on one man,
              Is taken as a slight by our new guests.

JOCASTA: Go tell the king his counsel has been heard.

CRETHEUS: Madame, I shall. (*he bows and goes*)

OEDIPUS: You'd better go make converse with the king,
              Lest he suspects our friendship goes too far.

JOCASTA: He will not think it wrong,
              His mind's too full of boys to care for me.

182

OEDIPUS: We cannot take that risk.

JOCASTA: Oh Oedipus,
              You think I'll let him come between us now,
              After all the love we shared last night?
              You brought me joy, and soothed my aching heart,
              Filled up my empty womanhood with bliss.
              I will not let that go without a fight.

OEDIPUS: I did not mean to part you from my bed,
              But only from my side.
              Discretion is the master of this art,
              And we should hold Him so,
              Not flaunt our love before your husband's eyes.

JOCASTA: I'll flaunt it how I wish. (*she waves and smiles at Laius*)
              Why should I hide my joy?
              Too long I've been the scapegoat to his ploy!

OEDIPUS: Desist from this!
              When'er we come within your husband's sight
              The coldness of your heart comes howling through,
              As if your icy hate would freeze him dead.
              These cruel and unprovoked verbose attacks
              Upon this man (whom I have greatly wronged)
              Cool my ardour, fan me with your hate,
              And cause me to have doubts our love is real.

JOCASTA: Oh cast these childish doubts from out your brain.
              I rail against this man with ice cold hate
              Because your fiery love has thawn my heart,
              And melted all those feelings, too long froze.
              But do not take offence,
              For like a bowl that runs its biased course,
              Then rights itself when it has hit the mark,
              So will my old resentment rage and rail,
              Until I have discharged this heap of woe,
              And righted once again my fragile love.
              In this I need your love to give me strength.
              My hate for Laius soon will run its course,
              So do not fear my tongue,
              For women strike their foes with angry words,
              While men, too often, end them with their swords.

OEDIPUS: Then keep these words in counsel with yourself,

183

For I no longer wish to be their foil.

LYSIAS: Your friend seems very taken with the queen.

CHRYSIPPUS: Besotted I would say.
He has not left her side since first he came.
Though I am sure they mean no coarse offence.

LYSIAS: In this I'm sure you're right,
Though they should err towards the cautious side,
For Laius is a fearful, jealous man.

(suddenly Arrian lets out a scream because Atreus has given her a love bite.)

ARRIAN: *(screams)* Ahhhh!
You've bit me on the neck.

ATREUS: I'll bite you lower down if you'll keep still.

(they fight playfully)

PELOPS: *(jumps up)* Those boys!
(whispers angrily to Hippodamia)
[Go! Keep them in their place.
I knew we should have made them stay at home.]

LAIUS: *(to Pelops)* Be not dismayed, there's no harm done.
They have their mother's fondness for good sport,
[*aside to Proteus*]
[And no doubt sell their favours cheaply too.]
(Proteus stifles a laugh)

(Hippodamia glares at Laius and then crosses to Arrian.)

HIPPODAMIA: Boys, boys,
Control your youthful spirits for a while.
Be tame today that you may soon be free.
Livia, a word.

LIVIA: Yes mam.

(they move aside)

HIPPODAMIA: That man has boiled my blood to overflow.
All through this day he's hinted at our plots,

184

Which failed through his vile treachery and fear!
I will not be so mocked,
For Lucien shall have his just revenge!
Ooh!

(She swoons. Livia catches her. The Watchman starts forward.)

LIVIA: Madam are you ill?

HIPPODAMIA: No no. Tis but a thought.
Poor Lucien, his name affects me so.
I thought I saw him here.

LIVIA: But madam, he is dead.

HIPPODAMIA: To think we sat through dinner with a man
Who took away the life of him I loved.
Revenge will have its day.

LIVIA: Madam, be still, you'll aggravate your heart.

HIPPODAMIA: Oh Lucien, I miss your gentle touch,
And long to have you here to ease my ache.
But no.
My cause is lost! My hope of life dispersed,
And scattered to the wind like so much chaff.
I am undone,
A broken straw that's blown where e're it will,
And is no longer master of its fate!
The power I sought to gain now drains away,
And leaves me like a bankrupt on Life's shore,
To be the jest and jibe of every fool!
O Lucien,
Where will I find fresh comfort now you're gone?

LIVIA: Madam. It does not do to dwell upon such thoughts.

HIPPODAMIA: Yes. Yes. I know too well. I'll reign my fury in,
Until such time as I can let it ride,
And trample into dust my deadly foes.
You have the phial?

LIVIA: I do.

HIPPODAMIA: Then keep it safe.
This night its sleeping draught will do good work,

185

And rid us of this king I've come to curse.
Go back to my sons and keep control,
Old Pelops moans and whines about their games.
His impotent old age begins to tell,
And shows him for the fool he has become.
Tis time, he too, began to think of death,
For soon he'll sleep a sound and dreamless sleep,
Which never shall have waking as its end.
But hush! We'll speak of this anon.

(She returns to King Pelops' side.)

ARRIAN: Your mother frets too greatly o'er your life.

ATREUS: She loves me. Why should she not show care?
               At least she knows true worth when it appears.

ARRIAN: You haughty brat!
               You are not worth the smallest thought I have.

LIVIA: Be still you two! Remember where we are!
               Your mother is a proud and noble queen,
               And does not wish her sons to bring her shame.

THYESTES: Ha!
               Our mother is a gorgon without love,
               Who has too much Ambition in her blood,
               Which overflows and stains all those around,
               Tainting them with her disordered woes.

LIVIA: Be silent fool! You know not what you say!
               We're in a foreign camp.
               Such jests will not be taken in good faith.

THYESTES: Who's making jests? I mean just what I say!

LYSIAS: Did you mark how Hippodamia swooned?

CHRYSIPPUS: I marked it well.
               She's ill and should be wrapped up in her bed.
               My father was unkind to let her come.

LYSIAS: They say she has had visions from her past,
               Which haunt her sleepless nights with waking dreams,
               And rend the very senses from her mind.

CHRYSIPPUS: That may be true, she looks a haunted soul.
               See how she works and wracks her wedding ring,
               As if she'd pull the finger from her hand.

LYSIAS: She killed her former husband, so they say,
               And further say she has designs on you,
               And hopes to make an end of your sweet life.

CHRYSIPPUS: She is a woman giv'n to wild extremes,
               Her temp'rament will rise or quickly fall
               As current thoughts dictate her current moods.
               She plotted once to have my life removed
               As also did she plot to kill the King,
               And Oedipus my friend. But we survived.

LYSIAS: That woman is insane if this be true!

CHRYSIPPUS: Tired and lonely, full of Life's cruel knocks,
               And greatly over-zealous for her sons.
               Perhaps that is insane, perhaps tis not?
               Or maybe she's more passionate than most,
               Who feel these self-same things but let them lie,
               And thus deny their passion any scope.
               I do not know, but pity her estate,
               And think she needs my love, more than my hate?

LYSIAS: Chastised once more.
               The essence of your dream perfumes your being,
               And saturates your thinking with kind thoughts
               Exuding true compassion to the air.
               Oh Chrysippus,
               I am no worthy pupil to your skill.

CHRYSIPPUS: And I no worthy tutor to your love.
               So do not deem me so.
               But strive to keep your mind alert and free,
               And do not judge too harshly what you see.

OEDIPUS: You cannot mean you're jealous of the boy!
               But he and I are friends!

JOCASTA: I know the sort of 'friends' that Laius keeps.

OEDIPUS: Oh woman keep your jealousy in check!
               This day has seen the gamut of your rage.
               First Laius and now Chrysippus as well.

187

	Are you so insecure that you must fear Every other friendship that you see? I shall not let you down. Why should I turn to him when I have you? And anyway, he has no need of me, For he enjoys the pleasures of the king.
JOCASTA:	They will not last him long! The king goes through these boys like hungry wolves Who kill more meat than they have need to eat. He'll soon be cast aside, for some new joy.
OEDIPUS:	That will not be! I shall not see it so! For Laius will make answer with his life, If he so much as harm that gentle boy.
JOCASTA:	Then what of me? Should Laius not make answer with his life, For all the harm that I have long endured? Or is our love so worthless in your eyes, That you would not take life to prove it true?
OEDIPUS:	I have no need to prove my love to you, More than, through last night's actions, I have done. So do not boil my anger in this way, Or question my sincerity in this.
LAIUS:	JOCASTA!
JOCASTA:	Lo. He calls.
LAIUS:	Jocasta, come and join us by our throne, Our regal guests are starved of your effects.
OEDIPUS:	Do as he says, I'll mingle with the crowd.
JOCASTA:	No. Come with me. I need your comfort yet.
LAIUS:	(*to Pelops*) We do intend to change our laws once more, For Chrysippus has had a mystic dream, Which shows the very nature of our world, To be completely other than it seems...

(*Suddenly Arrian lets out a shriek and Atreus chases her
knocking some wine jugs off the table. Pelops jumps up furious.*)

188

PELOPS: *(to Hippodamia)* Oh keep them in their place!
                   I said they should not come.
                   They know no more of etiquette than swine!

HIPPODAMIA: *(very loudly)* MY CHILDREN ARE NOT SWINE!

                   (silence! the whole room stares at her)

PELOPS: (hissing) Be silent wife! You know not where we are.

HIPPODAMIA: *(to Pelops)* You shall not mock my sons and 'scape unscathed!

PELOPS: My wife is feeling ill. We shall retire at once.
                   We thank you for a most delightful day.
                   Goodnight to all and may this peace live long.

                   (he bows and crosses to Chrysippus)

                   Goodnight my son, your mother is not well.
                   This journey has been made in too much haste,
                   And brings her fever on.

CHRYSIPPUS: Goodnight father.
                   A restful night will see her fit and well.

                   (Pelops kisses Chrysippus goodnight and exits.)

HIPPODAMIA: *(aside)* He shall not mock my sons and live to breathe!
                   Livia.

LIVIA: *(curtsies)* Mam.

HIPPODAMIA: Bring in that phial wherein my poison sleeps,
                   Now wakes the task for which their slumber keeps.

LIVIA: Yes mam.

                   *(Thyestes, Livia, Arrian, Atreus, the Watchman and
                   Hippodamia all exit followed by Proteus.)*

LAIUS: A lively pair.
                   Your father has great spirit for his age.

CHRYSIPPUS: Oh do not mock.
                   I wish he'd never made that hapless match.

(*Jocasta and Oedipus approach*)

JOCASTA: You called my dear?

LAIUS: Indeed I did.
You were the honoured hostess of this night,
But lavished all your favours on this man!
Had you been more attentive to your dues,
This... This ugly scene may well have been denied.

JOCASTA: I thought it meet to keep myself reserved,
As this was more a night to relish kings.

LAIUS: You sir,
You seem unduly friendly with my wife.

OEDIPUS: Your wife and I are friends, this much is true,
I did not think such friendship out of place,
And meant no form of insult to your crown.

LAIUS: Then take yourself indoors,
You tread upon the probity of guest,
And make yourself unwelcome to our eyes.

OEDIPUS: You go to far! I'll not be ruled in this.
I'm not some child to scold as you see fit.

LAIUS: You question my command?

OEDIPUS: I do when it o'ersteps its proper reach.

LAIUS: I will not be so baited in my court!

OEDIPUS: Nor I so lightly mocked by your foul tongue.

LAIUS: Then feel the mighty fury of my sword. (*he draws his sword.*)

JOCASTA: (*screams*) Ahh!

OEDIPUS: And you, mine! (*he draws his sword.*)

CRETHEUS: Protect the king!

(*Cretheus and the soldiers draw their swords and step forward.*)

LAIUS: Back. I'll deal with this alone.

190

(Jocasta approaches Laius.)

JOCASTA: Put up your sword!
              This man is but a guest within our court.
              Your jealousy has made your senses mad.

(Laius pushes Jocasta aside.)

LAIUS: Tis you who're mad to break faith with your king!

(Laius and Oedipus are about to set to when Chrysippus steps between them.)

CHRYSIPPUS: Laius! Oedipus!
              Are you intent to spoil this day of peace,
              By acting out a fresh and bloody war?

OEDIPUS: Step not between. This man insults my life,
              And will shed blood to pay for this foul fault.

CHRYSIPPUS: Put up these swords!
              For too much wine has addled both your minds,
              And shows you for the beasts you have become.
              Oedipus. Laius.

(they put up their swords)

LAIUS: True. True.
              The wine has kindled madness in our brains,
              And this long day worn patience to a thread.
              I did you wrong to think you'd caused offence.

OEDIPUS: As I did you.
              My temper rides so finely on its edge,
              It sometimes overspills before I know't.
              Here, take my hand,
              And seal our mutual friendship in its clasp.

LAIUS: And you this.
              We'll pardon by this act our hasty thoughts,
              Which over-rode true Courtesy's estate.

(they shake hands)

(to all) Friends, neighbours, countrymen of Thebes,

This day has ta'en its heavy toll on all,
And stretched our weary senses out of shape.
Let's to our beds,
And send our thoughts to sleep with peaceful dreams.
Lest we destroy the vantage we have gained.
I bid you all, goodnight.

VARIOUS: Goodnight. Farewell.

(they all exit apart from Chrysippus and Laius.)

LAIUS: Oh Chrysippus,
I feel your censure, say not one word more.
I'm in the wrong to lose my temper so,
And with this one who is your special friend.

CHRYSIPPUS: I have no wish to censure or chastise,
But rather, would outline my latest scheme,
Envisaged in that rare and precious dream,
And how we might attain its glorious end.
But come. Let's to our bed.
I see this fight still weights upon your head.

(they exit)

END OF ACT 5 SCENE 1

ACT 5 SCENE 2

Night. A cave, lit by some flares stuck in the wall. Nileus is asleep on the floor Tiresias is standing beside him, a strong wind blowing without. Tiresias appears to be listening to something, he then shakes Nileus.

TIRESIAS: Come! Tis time for us to go.
               Draw on your cloak, and leave these flares to glow,
               Our presence is demanded down below.

               (*Nileus rises and puts on his cloak.*)

NILEUS: Where are we going, and why, in such a storm?

TIRESIAS: We go to see the coming of the morn,
               And welcome in, its rare and precious light,
               Which will in time, put paid to this dark night.
               But come, we tarry here too long,
               Tis high time we were on the road and gone.

               (*they exit*)

                    END OF ACT 5 SCENE 2

ACT 5 SCENE 3

Before Chrysippus' bed chamber.

(*Enter Laius and Chrysippus shortly after the end of scene 1 debating.*)

LAIUS: I think in time this nation shall be great,
And spread its wisdom far beyond these shores.

CHRYSIPPUS: No.
For as it stands, with Man the way he is,
Our nation is no better or no worse,
Than all the other nations here around.
At best, the raw potential for new hope,
But if, through true example, and good laws,
Our people see the pathway they must tread,
And work to overcome their base desires,
Transform themselves into a purer being,
And make compassion active in the world:
Then Greece will blaze a beacon in Life's night,
And fill the world with Inspiration's light
Shining out through Time for all Mankind.
And you will be Philosophy's true king,
Putting into practice through your deeds,
The perfect Way of Life: The Good: The True:
Thus showing Man what he was born to do.

LAIUS: Bravo! (*he applauds*)
What wonders will you shower upon us next?
This is a mighty vision you uphold,
And one that will take time to implement,
But I have faith that what you say is true,
And one day may be manifest on earth.
And these new laws, fresh drafted in your hand,
Will guide the steps of those who tread that way.

(*enter Proteus*)

But look, here comes a man with business on his mind.
Good Proteus! What news?

PROTEUS: The storm renews its fury now it's night,

194

And seems to blow as if the world would end,
And hurl our snow-topped mountains to the sea.
But they are all abed.
Pelops and his queen are fast asleep,
And snore like fatted pigs awaiting death.
Their sep'rate chambers shake with equal force,
Vibrating to the rhythm of their breath.

LAIUS: The others?

PROTEUS: Their maid took in some off'ring for the king,
              And then went off to nestle with the son
              Whose sour-faced looks, and hang-dog surly moods,
              Make all our ugly hags seem precious queens.
              The other maid is with the younger son,
              Both tasting blissful sport in sweat drenched dreams.
              The only one not yet asleep in bed,
              Is but a twisted wreck of human shape,
              Their Watchman, so distorted and deformed,
              He makes our rugged coastline seem quite straight.

LAIUS: Oh, that old fool! Why is he not asleep?

CHRYSIPPUS: I've heard he does not sleep,
              But counts away the minutes of the night,
              Pining o'er some unrequited love.

PROTEUS: That may well be.
              He paces up and down like one possessed,
              His twisted legs loud-beating on the floor,
              And clacking out his own distorted time.
              I've put a younger man to watch his tread,
              And wake me if he wanders from that room.

LAIUS: Good. Get you to your bed.
              This was a service handled with great care,
              Tomorrow I will show you, our reward.

PROTEUS: Goodnight, good sirs.

LAIUS: Goodnight.

CHRYSIPPUS: Goodnight. Sleep well.

              (*exit Proteus*)

LAIUS: Well, young pup, it seems our worry's through.
All threats upon your life have now resolved,
And settled into one untroubled sleep.
Come, our chamber waits.

(he puts his arm round Chrysippus and laughs)

Tomorrow we shall view this world afresh,
And you shall show the way to make Greece great.

*(They enter the inner chamber which serves as a bedroom. the
lights dim to show the passing of time. we hear only the howling
of the wind, the crack of lightning and the thunder's distant
roar.)*

END OF ACT 5 SCENE 3

ACT 5 SCENE 4

Before Chrysippus' bed chamber.

(*Enter Hippodamia with a torch, followed by Thyestes with a sword and Atreus*)

HIPPODAMIA: You have the sword?

THYESTES: How many times must I assure you? Yes!

HIPPODAMIA: Good.
This night will see the death of that foul fiend,
Who comes between your persons and the throne?

THYESTES: What?

ATREUS: What do you mean?
You said you heard some animal in pain,
And roused us from our sleep that we should help,
Not cause the death of some poor helpless being.

HIPPODAMIA: Sweet foolish child, your head is free from guile.
Come to my arms. Come. Come. Both.
(*she hugs them both*)
My darling offspring, angels of my womb,
Progenitors of our ennobled race.
Tonight you must put off your childish ways,
And don the cloak of manhood that is yours.
Within this world there's only one true law,
And that is: "always grasp the thing you want",
For no one else will give you what you need.
I learnt this lesson young,
And put it into practice all my youth,
And now you have the chance to do the same.
I said I'd call upon you in the night,
To do my special bidding, in some deed.
Do you not recall?

THYESTES: We do.

HIPPODAMIA: Well now's that time.
For, sleeping in that chamber lies the boy,

197

Who stands between you and your rightful throne,
And you must end his life to gain control,
Of all that is by heritage your due.

ATREUS: Who is this boy that bars our chance to rule?

HIPPODAMIA: Chrysippus, Pelops only son!

ATREUS: Chrysippus?

HIPPODAMIA: Yes Chrysippus,
The true and rightful heir of these estates.
But take this sword and make your passion known,
Dash him away and Thebes will be your own!

THYESTES: You want us to kill Chrysippus?

HIPPODAMIA: Of course! Are you still half asleep,
And think you can but dream yourself to power?
Go. Do it now, before the castle wakes.
Just end his life and you are free to reign,
Become what my proud destiny desires,
And reach the heights to which your blood aspires.
But hush,
I'll test their chamber, check your route is clear,
Wait silent here, until I re-appear.

(*Hippodamia hands the torch to Atreus and approaches the door of the chamber to listen.*)

THYESTES: Our mother's mad! we must not do this deed.
Her mind has gone beyond all hope of cure.

ATREUS: She's mad indeed! But what has made her so?
I have not heard her rave like this before,
Nor seen her act with such a wild intent.

THYESTES: Are your eyes blind when all the world can see?
Our mother has been toiling o'er this plot
Since first we came to sojourn here in Greece,
And would have had her way had not her child,
Been still-born in her dark and festering womb,
And thrown the flimsy balance of her mind.

ATREUS: A child! What Child? What ghastly jape is this?

198

THYESTES: This is no jape, but words of ice cold truth.
               She had a child to Lucien, who's dead,
               And later when his child too, came to die,
               It drove all sense of sanity awry,
               And left her like some wretched waif and stray,
               Raving in her sorrow and dismay,
               And screaming for revenge upon the world.

ATREUS: No! You lie!
               What proof is there of this? I knew of no such child?
               You're out to gain this kingdom for yourself!
               She had no still-born child in Lucien's name.
               This is some wicked scheme to steal her love,
               And part me from the birthright that I'm due.

THYESTES: Do you despise me so,
               To think I'd stoop to such a feeble trick?

ATREUS: Where your desires turn on the hope of rule,
               I'd trust your love no further than a cur.

THYESTES: Then hate me, for I speak naught but the truth.

ATREUS: I'll hate you 'till you prove this lie is true.

THYESTES: Does she not prove this for me by her acts,
               Urging us to kill this gentle child.

ATREUS: She has our best intentions in her heart.
               For if he stands between us and the throne,
               Then we must take his life to earn our crown.
               Or else forever wallow in his wake.

THYESTES: Bah!
               D'you think we'd live to profit from this act?
               They'd have us in our graves before the Dawn,
               Had ope'd his sunny eyes to view the world.
               Are you so much infected by her love,
               That you can not see madness, plain and bold?
               But hush, she comes.

               (*Hippodamia returns*)

HIPPODAMIA: There's two of them, their breathing marks them so.
               It must be Laius sleeping with his boy.
               If he should wake, then take his life as well,

                              199

'Twill save my heavy potion extra work.
Go gently both, and make your actions swift,
Two blows will rid forever all your woes!

THYESTES: (*aside to Atreus*) [Is this not proof enough?]
No!
I shall not take his life, or any other life.
Your mind has been demented by your loss.
Go back to bed and take some sleeping draught.
Tomorrow we shall have a physic called,
And minister sweet potions to your head.

HIPPODAMIA: Physic? Loss? What random words are these?
Go in and do the deed.
D'you think I do not know how finely Fate,
Rides upon this moment we approach?
If we do not strike now,
The whole of Greece escapes our grasp for good!
Would you deny this climax to my life?

THYESTES: Yes.

HIPPODAMIA: Yes?
What answer's this from my own flesh and blood?
(*to Atreus*) And you, will you reply the same?

ATREUS: I... I... Mama, you do not seem yourself.
Go back to bed and sleep until the dawn,
And then we shall discuss the matter more.

HIPPODAMIA: Discuss it more! What girlish squeaks are these?
Go to! The hour is passing quick. And will not come again!

THYESTES: No! We shall not kill for you. You're mad,
And raving like the whore you have become.

(*Hippodamia slaps Thyestes very hard across the face he falls
to the ground and whimpers and whines.*)

Ahh!

ATREUS: Thyestes!

HIPPODAMIA: You vile ungrateful creature of my flesh,
To turn against this breast which gave you suck;
This womb which nurtured all your childish blood,

200

And held you in 'till you could bear the sun.
Is this my sole reward?
Have I endured my hellish life for this:
To be denied by those who drew my love,
And every ounce of strength that I attained?
Will you devour me now like some wild beast,
Who knows no sense of motherhood or pride,
But rips the very offspring from its womb?
Have I endured maternity for this?
No. No. This cannot be. I do not hear you right.

ATREUS: Mama. Let's go from here. Your senses are deranged.
This is no place to overthrow your heart.
Come, rest awhile, your fever will depart,
And we will bring you comfort and good love.

HIPPODAMIA: You too!
You turn against me in my hour of need,
And throw me to these wolves who rip my flesh?
(to Thyestes) Get up!
You weak and whimpering, worthless, wretched, scum!
Give me that sword. I'll show you how to kill!

(She grabs the sword and exits into the chamber)

THYESTES: Let's go. I want no part in this.

ATREUS: Nor I.
Our mother, like you say, has gone insane,
And chased all hope of succour from her brain.
Let's go, before this act is blamed on us.

(He moves to go then hesitate for a second.)

But wait! Chrysippus? Should we not spare his life,
And warn him 'fore her madness has its fill?

*(suddenly there is a loud blood-curdling scream from the bed
chamber)*

CHRYSIPPUS: *(off)* AHHHH!

THYESTES: His fate no longer rests within our will.
Look to yourself,
Only the gods can save his spirit now.

(they run off.)

LAIUS: *(off)* Murder! Bloody Murder! Guards! Guards!

(re-enter Hippodamia in a daze splattered in blood and carrying the bloodied sword.)

HIPPODAMIA: *(slowly)* The two of them abed like man and wife.
How gently did they sleep.
And how I longed to join them in that rest.
Such beauty on the face of one so young.
Then he awoke,
And saw me standing o'er him like some wraith,
Intent upon the evil of my deeds.
And he just smiled, a sweet and radiant smile,
A smile, forgiving all my former sins,
And purging me of all that I might do.
Then I brought down this sword upon his head,
Until that pretty visage was no more;
But old and wrinkled, splattered with his blood,
And dashed beyond all Recognition's art.
Oh wherefore did he smile?

(She drops the sword.)

Sweet child,
That you could bless me kindly in this way,
While I had naught but hatred on my mind.
Oh such a sweet and saving, caring, smile,
Haunting me like visions from my past.
Oh Father, wherefore art thou going?
I'll come and gather lilacs for the dead.
Don't leave me here so cold. My children all are gone,
Dissolved in blood and blaming me for life.
Peeweet. Peeweet.
I hear the lapwing's call. They are my friends.
And draw me to their nest.
Oh, can't you hear them father? Look. They fly,
So sweetly and so brightly in the sky.
Peeweet. Peeweet. Lead on. Lead on.
I'll come to join with you my feathered friends,
And we will soar together to our ends.

(She exits lightly, following the birds, as Laius enters carrying the dead body of Chrysippus in his arms.)

202

LAIUS: (*shouting after Hippodamia*)
               Woman! See this dreadful tragedy you own!

               (*He places Chrysippus gently on the ground and kneels beside*
       him.)

               Oh child of Nature's bounty overflow'n.
               Deprived, deserted, dead, in one cruel blow!
               What would I give to change this breath for yours.
               What can it mean,
               That one so kind and gentle in his ways,
               Could be deprived by one who's so depraved?
               Oh crack ye walls of flesh that dam these tears,
               Throw open every sluice and let salt flow!
               What is this life that takes away such gifts
               And lets such ugly carnivores survive?
               Sweet child.
               No epitaph can speak your praise enough,
               No words I say can do the justice due,
               To all the vast perfection of your being.
               Oh why did this occur? Such savage act!
               Such brutal inhumanity to man,
               Depriving me of all I've ever loved.
               What man alive can live if this be Life?
               See how these gashes let your blood flow free,
               Blood that was awash with boundless love,
               But now contains no trace of you at all.
               What monstrous joke is this to take away,
               The only source of beauty I have known,
               And turn it into this inhuman mass,
               And empty shell, a carcass of decay?
               Oh gods, that you should let him end this way!

               (*He holds Chrysippus head in his arms and kisses him*)

               (*enter Oedipus*)

OEDIPUS: (*to himself*) What wretched sight is this?
               You bloody butcher! Slaughterer of lambs!
               Do you devour the flesh wherein love lies?
               Is this how you reward the one's you've loved?

LAIUS: You!
               Vain creature, who would part me from my wife,
               Do you come now to settle our last rage?
               Then timely come,

For I have need to vent my Fury's spleen,
And you will serve to purge me of my ire!

(He picks up the sword which is lying there, Oedipus draws his own sword.)

OEDIPUS: Go to't fiend!
That you could be the parent of such doom,
And waste so eas'ly that, which man should love.

LAIUS: Come at me boy, I'm ready for your blood.
We'll settle here, who has the greatest love.

(they fight.)

OEDIPUS: Take that old man.

(he stabs him.)

Go find that place in hell which holds your name.

LAIUS: AHHH! Help! I die. Help! Assassins! Help!

(He dies on the ground near Chrysippus.)

(Oedipus kneels beside Chrysippus)

OEDIPUS: Sweet youth.
What had you done to warrant such an end?
How strangely I'm unmoved by your cruel death.
Has war so drained the feeling from my blood,
That I no longer suffer at your loss,
Or grieve to lose the vision I perceived?
And yet,
The passing of this man, whom I loved not,
Has sent some strange vibration through my frame,
Which gnaws me, like some illness in the brain,
That will not let sweet thoughts arise again.

(Enter Jocasta wearing her shawl. [see act i scene 3.])

JOCASTA: Oh!
What mischief feeds this lie unto my eyes,
My husband, and his paramour - both dead?

(she puts her hand on Oedipus' shoulder)

204

Oh Oedipus, what slaughters happened here?

OEDIPUS: I know not what befell,
For Chrysippus was dead when I arrived.
So I then took revenge upon the king. See there,
His wretched cowardly sword still steeped in blood.

JOCASTA: That is not his sword.
Tis one that old King Pelops wore last night,
To grace the royal splendour of our feast!

OEDIPUS: Then Hippodamia's had her evil way!
The curse she strove to prove has held its sway,
And battered out the life of those we loved!

(Jocasta looks at the body of Laius.)

JOCASTA: I think, had you been absent, I would weep,
To see the man I loved so dead and cold,
Regardless that our life was one long hell.
But you have filled my heart with such warm love,
That I feel nothing for him but contempt,
And joy, that you and I are both now free,
To wed together, live the life we choose,
And show the world the splendour of our love.

OEDIPUS: I know not what I feel.
Except this endless drumming of dull pain,
Which beats a hollow echo through my brain.
My friend is dead, and too, my new-made king,
And with them all my hope of future time.
I feel that I have lost all sense of past,
Been severed from the roots that once were mine,
And now have nothing left to call my own.
I'm in a limbo, void of any life,
And must drift here in this unfigured state,
Until these actions work their terror out.
For life is but a fragment of some whole,
Which we, in our dumb ignorance ignore,
Thinking that we can, by present acts,
Be guiltless of our actions in the past.
Oh vanish clouds. My mind's confused,
And cannot fit clear reason to its thought.
I feel that I have lost some part of me,
But know not why, or what this part might be.

205

I hear the words of Delphi's sacred sage,
Ringing like a curse within my brain,
But know not how to rid me of this pain.

JOCASTA: Come.
Shake these morbid shadows from your head,

(*pointing to the dead bodies*)

We'll bury thoughts like that, along with these.
Look to your new estate and cherish that,
For we shall take what needful time is due,
To honour and to mourn our royal dead,
Then marry for the sake and weal of Thebes.
And you shall play the king to my proud queen,
And we shall rule this land like none before.
Does this not thrill your mind and please your heart?
What's this?
You shiver like a wind-entangled leaf?
Poor sickly child, throw off this sorrow now.
Here,

(*Jocasta wraps her shawl around Oedipus' shoulders.*)

Put on my shawl, and keep your body warm,
It will revive the spirit in your blood,
And fill you with the courage to go on.

(*She pulls his head to her stomach.*)

Rest here awhile, in silence and in peace,
And taste the soothing comfort of my love.
This day, though sad, has brought us both great joy.

(*Enter Proteus. He stops, stunned*)

PROTEUS: Hell's blood! What slaughter has occurred?

JOCASTA: T'was Hippodamia's curse!
She's slain the one's we loved.
Both Chrysippus, and Laius our dear spouse.

PROTEUS: No!
I knew I never should have left her side,
That viper slithers death where're she goes.
Oh my dread King,

206

That I should be so careless with your life...

JOCASTA: No.
Do not blame yourself. There's nothing you could do.
Her evil is no match for humankind.

PROTEUS: Then stop your ears, for I have more to tell.

JOCASTA: Oedipus, arise. There is worse news to come,
And you must bear the brunt, for I am weak.
Stand you in my stead 'till Thebes is well.

(Whispered to Oedipus) [Oedipus, arise I say.]

OEDIPUS: *(to Jocasta)* [I do not have the stomach for such work.]

JOCASTA: *(whispered to Oedipus)*
[Reign in your fears! Tis women should look sick,
And men give strength and courage by their lead.
Arise, and bear the burden of your role.]

(she helps Oedipus up.)

OEDIPUS: Say on.
Our heart is full of grief and want's no more,
But we shall hear the horrors you must tell,
And execute the duty of our role.

PROTEUS: Pelops has been murdered by her too.

OEDIPUS: Ye gods! Is there no justice in this world?
How was this taken off?

PROTEUS: His nightcap drink of milk, sad kiss of death,
Which lay half-drunk beside his silent bed,
Was laced with deadly poison from a phial,
Which we found, scarcely hidden, in her room.

OEDIPUS: But how was it applied?

PROTEUS: T'was taken in to him, with loving care,
By Livia, the elder of those maids,
Before the lenient witness of these eyes!

OEDIPUS: Ye gods!
This woman's fury knows no earthly bounds!

207

Stop her! At all cost have her found,
Before she does more outrage to this house!

(*enter Cretheus with other servants*)

OEDIPUS: What news?
Although our ears now dread to hear much more.

CRETHEUS: Both her sons are fled,
Made off with those two whores who served the queen.

OEDIPUS: Then where is she?

CRETHEUS: There has been no report.

OEDIPUS: Scourge the grounds! She must not slip away.
That woman is a sorceress from hell!

(*Exit Cretheus and Proteus, some of the other servants stay behind. Lysias enters, he walks slowly and calmly towards the bodies.*)

JOCASTA: Look.
Here comes a heart that Sorrow's yet to break.

LYSIAS: Oh Laius, my sweet king, what here befell?

JOCASTA: T'was Hippodamia's guile, bereft his life.

LYSIAS: How unbecoming Death sits on your head,
His bloody crown disfigures your kind face,
And makes a frozen waste of all your love.
Break heart,
And shed those cool wet tears of needful grief,
For you have lost a true and valued friend.

(*he turns away and weeps*)

JOCASTA: What's wrong? He turns away.
He has not seen that Chrysippus is dead.
Go you gently to him, break the news,
Before his sorrow robs him of all sense.

OEDIPUS: Lysias,
Draw more salt to your eyes and look again,
For see you not that Chrysippus is dead!

LYSIAS: Oh say not so. For Chrysippus lives still!
            This gouged and tortured flesh that we see here,
            Is but the outward shell of his great heart,
            Which beats beyond the confines of this form,
            Eludes the clammy grasp of icy Death,
            And lives to bless the world with countless wealth.
            For he's become, what he has always been,
            The guardian of Compassion in this realm,
            And even now is show'ring us with love,
            And raining down his virtue from above.
            For he's the very air that gives us breath;
            The sunlight, spreading warmth across the earth;
            The vibrant flower, that cheers our saddened heart;
            The rainbow, that appears when storms depart.
            He is the silver moon which sends us light,
            To guide us through the darkness of the night:
            The cooling rain, that swells the willing fruit,
            Or buries deep to slake the thirsty root;
            And too, the prodding bee, who sucks the juice,
            And stimulates the flower to reproduce.
            He is, the sweetest sound that can be heard,
            Those made by human voice, or chirping bird;
            And when men seek to delve into their mind,
            He is the richest treasure they can find.
            For he's each act of Goodness we attain,
            And every kindly thought that we contain,
            While Beauty, is the language of his deeds,
            Rewarding, through its splendour, all our needs.
            So say not so, that Chrysippus is dead,
            For by this bloody sight you've been misled,
            So shake off thoughts of Hate, and banish Greed,
            And join him, in his unexampled creed.
            For he lives on, beyond us, and above,
            Uniting all mankind in his pure love.

OEDIPUS: Oh bravely said! No other words would do.
            This was the fitting tribute to our friend.
            Take them up and bury them in state.
            We'll honour them with all the rituals due.

            (Some servants move forward to gather up the dead when the
            Watchman enters carrying the dead Hippodamia in his arms,
            flanked by Proteus and Cretheus.)

209

What's this? Is Hippodamia found?

WATCHMAN: She's here.
Dead and broken, smashed beyond repair.

OEDIPUS: A fate too good for one so wholly bad.

WATCHMAN: Chew in your tongue! She was not wholly bad.
But one who shouldered cares beyond her scope.
She was a woman, and a mother too,
And held too rich a feeling for her sons,
Who threw away the love she freely gave,
Deserted her and chased her to her grave.
I loved her! And I will not hear her mocked.
She was not bad, just thwarted in her hopes.
And had more heart than any of you knew.

(he goes forward and lays her on the ground)

For though I'm crippled, twisted, and deformed,
Here lies the only soul who showed me love,
More bent and broke than ever I have been.

OEDIPUS: Find some other place to lay her down,
She has no right to grace such hallowed ground.

WATCHMAN: She has the right of every human being!
Are you so good, that you have done no wrong?

OEDIPUS: Then tell us how she died?
Her death may yet shine favour on her life.

WATCHMAN: I heard the awful wailings from this room,
And saw her rushing past like one insane,
Deluded by the phantoms from her brain.
She claimed she saw the lapwings flying high,
And calling her to join them in the sky,
That she might soar above her endless pain,
And be a carefree child with them again.
I followed her, to see where she would lead,
And save her, lest she do herself some harm,
Or need some help to free her from this charm.
Her step was light, her face was fresh and pure.
Her eyes - ablaze like beacons on a hill -
Shone out and saw her feathered friends alone.

210

T'was if some smiling visage from on high,
Beckoned her to join them in the sky.
For, like some child out running through the fields,
She skipped onto the parapet above
And, lifting up her hands like silver wings,
Leapt into the air to hear them sing.
I stood there, like a man bereft of life,
Clutching at the space where she had been,
While tears of sadness flooded from my eyes,
And wished they had not seen what they had seen.
She hovered for a moment in that air,
Crying like a peeweet to the sky,
And flew beyond the evil of this world,
Happy that her hour had come to die.
Then Chrysippus appeared, his smiling face,
Filling all the vastness of that space,
And took her up within his gentle arms,
To lead her far away from Life's cruel charms.
And as her spirit soared above the clouds,
Released at last from that great weight of woe,
Her soft and tender body hit the ground,
Dashed to mushy pulp like driven snow.
Then in these hapless arms I brought her hence,
That I might shed these tears in her defence.

OEDIPUS: Bravo old man, your speech has won our hearts.
Let her be buried bravely like the rest.

(*enter Tiresias and Nileus*)

OEDIPUS: What brings you here, you crusty worthless scum,
Sniffing like some vulture round this cull?
You've come too late; the tragedy is done.

TIRESIAS: Huh! Your tragedy has only just begun.
I gave you ample warning on that hill,
But you refused to heed my sage advice.
Observe this chaos well,
For this black day will dog you all your life!

OEDIPUS: Begone! You are not welcome here!
Go take your sightless warnings somewhere else.

TIRESIAS: I have not come for you, but for the boy.
His body's due to find a guilt free home,
More fitting to the nature of his life.

OEDIPUS: What!
              You'd even try to rob us of our dead?

TIRESIAS: Don't be afeared. You'll soon be making more.
              The Pythian curse has only just begun.

OEDIPUS: Go hence! Remove yourself from here.
              And never let me see your face again.

TIRESIAS: They'll come a time when you will crave my sight!
              Lysias.

LYSIAS: Yes?

TIRESIAS: Take up the body. You will come with us.

LYSIAS: I?

              (*Nileus goes forward*)

NILEUS: Do as he says t'was Chrysippus' wish.

LYSIAS: Chrysippus?

NILEUS: Yes. Come. We'll teach you in good time,
              For you have drunk his vision to the full.

              (*Nileus and Lysias take up the body of Chrysippus.*)

OEDIPUS: Stop!

JOCASTA: Oh let them go,
              He's more akin to their likes than our own.
              We have sufficient dead to grieve and mourn.

TIRESIAS: Farewell.
              Your minds are not prepared for freedom yet.
              Until this evil consequence is o'er,
              You'll recreate this hell for aeons more.

OEDIPUS: Begone!
              And save your scabrous curses for yourself!

              (*Tiresias exits following the corpse of Chrysippus.*)

Take up our dead and bear them to their graves,
This day has seen great tragedy occur.

(*he takes hold of Jocasta's hand*)

Come,
We'll praise the gods, that they will keep us free,
For we shall join in strength to guarantee,
Such outrage never blights this house again!

END OF ACT 5 SCENE 4

END OF ACT FIVE

THE END

Milton Keynes UK
Ingram Content Group UK Ltd.
UKHW020802241123
433194UK00016B/1023